Recipe for the TENNIS Player's SOUL

By Dave Rineberg

Frederick Fell Publishers, Inc.

2131 Hollywood Boulevard, Suite 305

Hollywood, Florida 33020

954-925-5242

e-mail: fellpub@aol.com

Visit our Web site at www.fellpub.com

Library of Congress Cataloging-in-Publication Data

Rineberg, Dave, 1965-
  Recipe for the tennis player's soul : a training guide for the new game / by Dave Rineberg.
     p. cm.
  ISBN 0-88391-117-5 (trade pbk. : alk. paper)
  1. Tennis. I. Title.
  GV995.R55 2004
  796.342--dc22

                              2004010307

ACKNOWLEDGEMENTS

How does anyone come to write a book that claims to have all the answers? In my case, this book, would not have been written if not for the constant requests and prodding by my former and current students/players to put my stroke techniques, fitness training methods and tennis beliefs down on paper. My deepest thanks goes out to each one of them who didn't mind sometimes being the subject of my experiments in my quest to create the perfect tennis player.

I would like to thank my publisher Frederick Fell for all their hard work in taking all my years of scribbled notes and turning them into this wonderful book.

I would also like to thank Brian Thomas for writing the foreword to this book to get you the reader off to a great start.

I would like to thank model Brittany Wagner for her great photographs that make all the strokes and shots in this book more beautiful.

And special Thanks to Coach Dave Rempel for all his advice, input and photographic style.

AUTHOR'S NOTES

The recipe for becoming a successful tennis player in the New Game is all but simple. You'll need to have the hand eye ability to return serves at speeds of up to150mph, the quickness to chase down laser-like ground strokes hit into the deepest corners of the court, be mentally tough enough to stick to your game plan for three to five hours per match and then have the endurance to wake up and do it all over again the next day.

Yes the game has come a long way from the days of old when the men wore long pants and the ladies wore dresses. Back then the recipe for success might have been as simple as having the ball striking talent to hit a shot out of the reach of an opposing player. But just like any great recipe over the years someone adds something to it or changes it in a way that makes it better. It's now a game that requires a player to not only have great ball striking talent but also great athleticism.

Even since the days of Connors, Mac, Chrissie and Martina, which is when it is said the tennis boom took place bringing more people into this sport to: compete, improve their fitness level and just have fun, the game has change immensely. I can still remember watching Connors change sides of the net and drink an entire Coke before returning to play. That is unheard of in the New Game where many players have their own scientific concocted drinks that hydrate, fuel and energize them according to their particular body type.

So what does all this mean? It means that if you really want to become a tennis player playing at the highest levels of the New Game, you must be ready to dedicate yourself both physically and mentally to becoming the best you can be. And you need to start as early as possible!

For the past fifteen years I have had the privilege of coaching tennis in the most fertile breeding grounds in the world for tennis players, South Florida. Nowhere else in the world will you find such a plethora of tennis players ranging from the beginner level to the Professional all training with great intensity and focus, beneath a constant sun. In those years I have been fortunate to work with each and every type of these players (including seven years in which I coached the two best female players of the New Game, Venus and Serena Williams) and in doing so I tried numerous tactics and teaching methods to help bring the best out of each and every one of them, helping to guide them in their personal search for excellence in this game of mistakes.

The real truth is though, that only some players will succeed in their quest and indeed capture their dream of becoming tennis professionals, while others will not. Sometimes what is stopping a player from advancing is not their talent, but their lack of direction and knowledge about how to go about attaining their goals and dreams. I hope this book can help give those of you that are on that journey a possible path to follow towards your dreams. But even if your goals are not that lofty this book still has a lot to offer you in your tennis development.

I must tell you that this book is by no means the only way to play successful tennis. It is merely my recipe for such success. To include all my information though would be lengthy so I've stuck to what I believe to be the necessities. It's a break down of the latest stroke techniques and shots to own, off-court and on-court training methods, playing strategies and tactics, all with a little philosophy mixed throughout, that I believe you must have in order to compete successfully at the games highest level.

This book is written first for you the player; as it is up to what's inside you as to how good your ball striking and shot making skills will get and to how high up the world tennis ladder you will go. Secondly it is written for all the coaches and parents of players, who are traveling along that same path as you the player and who play a crucial role in the guiding and nurturing of a player's development. I hope it will be of use to all of you in the pursuit of your dreams.

Foreword

I've known coach Dave Rineberg for over a decade or so and couldn't agree more to his philosophy of how this game of ours is and indeed should be played and in which direction it is headed. I feel this is a very timely book that addresses the needs of players of all levels, coaches and parents of players who are all looking for guidance on what is a most difficult road.

There is no doubt that working hard is the essence of this game of tennis, although hard work can be an object lesson in futility without a tailor made plan. Recipe for a Tennis Player's Soul, provides your plan if indeed you have the desire to work hard.

Recipe for a Tennis Player's Soul, will give you direction towards your ultimate goal and a plan of action so your hard work can get you around obstacles you may not even be aware of. Instead of beating your head against technical, physical and strategic brick walls.

As with any good recipe, the ingredients must compliment each other and balance well in order to achieve a desired outcome, this book gives you that balance. It will answer all your questions, remove technical limitations, intrigue, exhaust and exhilarate you as you strive to play at the highest levels of this game. And in the end, it will guide you to the extent of your physical abilities and if you're really paying attention, it will take you beyond.

Coach Rineberg is very, a matter a fact, in his advice to you on what it takes to reach the highest levels of this game and unlike other instructional books that sometimes sugar coat or misrepresent how truly difficult this game of tennis is and what kind of dedication, discipline and desire it takes to reach the pro ranks, there is nothing but brutal honesty and directness in his recipe for success.

Best of luck!

Brian Thomas
Graduate Oxford
Former Tour Professional
Tennis Teacher and Coach

PREFACE

'OPPOSITE DAY'

As a coach I use to wonder why some of my practice sessions went smoothly and others were disastrous. How could a player have it all together one day and be totally out of it another day? Why, when no matter how you tried to communicate your message or lesson to your player, it just seemed it went in one ear and out the other? Frustrating scenarios sure, but to coaches everywhere my advice on those days, is not to get frustrated or doubt your coaching skills. Don't go back and rewrite your coaching philosophy or redo your drill book. The answer may be much simpler then you think. The answer may just be that it's, 'Opposite Day'.

In the early 90's, I was coaching two young girls, sisters, ages eleven and twelve, in the sport of tennis. They were phenoms in the sport and practicing every day for an eventual professional career. On this particular day, I

showed up at the tennis courts for practice at our usual time of 1:00pm, excited to begin incorporating a series of new drills that I had stayed up late nights working out the details.

I was all business back then, a little less flexible and a little more stubborn then I am now, although my current players will probably tell you different. I thought that every practice session should be about getting the maximum amount of effort out of my players in the two-hour allotted time slot. I thought that every minute of those two hours should be used to drill in the strokes and shots and focus intensely on the playing strategies and tactics of the game until it all became an unconscious act. I was about to learn that there were more things that I needed to consider. On this day I was the one who was going to get taught a lesson and I should have known something was up by the girls' initial greeting.

"Hi girls," I said as I walked up to the court.

"Bye," they answered.

I looked at them strangely and they turned towards

each other and giggled. I didn't have a clue at this point what was going on and just ignored the comment.

"Why don't you girls start up in the frontcourt today so we can work on volleys," I said as I walked to my side of the court. When I turned around the girls were in the back-court behind the baseline. Since that was where we normally started practices, I just figured they must not of heard me and so I began feeding in the balls to start our practice.

"Let's hit everything to the right side of the court for the first ten minutes," I said. But every ball I fed to them they hit to the left side. This time I figured there was just a misunderstanding of whose right side I had meant, so I continued. After ten minutes of hitting, I was ready to start some of my new drills.

After my first three drills failed to accomplish anything close to what I had planned, and it seemed the girls were giggling even more now then ever, I elected we take a break so they could get a drink and I could go back into my drill book to find something that they might understand better or might work right. As I was flipping through some

pages I asked if they would pass me one of the bottles of blue Gatorade in the ice chest. They handed me a Gatorade but it was a green one. I stared at them with a puzzled look and then asked for a towel. They handed me a hat. I tried again by asking for a tennis ball, they gave me a racquet and then burst into uncontrollable laughter.

I threw up my arms, "Ok I give up. What is going on?" I asked.

In between their laughter they got it out.

"It's Opposite Day!" they said in unison.

"Opposite Day? What is that, a new holiday?" I asked.

"That means whatever you say today we are going to do the opposite or the closest opposite we can. We planned it on the way over to the courts today."

The smile that had come across my face during their explanation had grown into a big ole Kansas grin by the time they finished. I sat and just shook my head at the realization that these two young students had just become the teachers. They had just taught their serious stubborn coach an important lesson to remember when coaching young people; one that I will never again forget.

That lesson was: Be prepared to adjust any practice you have planned, remember to keep it fun, and always be on the lookout for, 'Opposite Day'.

To this day, that lesson that I learned from those two giggling little girls is written at the top of my junior development drill book for all to see and to remind me of that reason we all started playing this game in the first place.

So just who were those two tennis phenoms who gave their coach a valuable lesson; you might know them by their first names: Venus & Serena.

Table of Contents

CHAPTER ONE

The Tennis Player Athlete

So you want to be tennis pro?

Are you sure? Because if you're not willing to work hard in your practices each and every day, to set realistic goals, to drill with discipline for hours at a time mastering the various strokes & shots, to sweat blood in preparing your body athletically for the tournament grind, to learn from your past failures and early successes, to deal with self placed pressure and pressures from every source around you, to make plans and then stick with your plans even when faced with difficulties or distractions, then I suggest you stop reading right now and take up an easier sport. But if your desire is strong to begin with, if you're willing to spend the countless hours needed in extreme heat busting your tail to learn the strokes and shots, if you have the guts and the gumption and the heart and soul to become a mentally tough competitor, then your chances of making it onto the pro tour are greatly improved. That's what it takes and that is what makes up the champions of this sport of tennis.

Believe it: To become a successful tennis professional in the New Game means you have to have the strength to return serves at speeds of up to150mph, the quickness to chase down laser-like ground strokes hit into the deepest corners of the court, be mentally tough enough to stick to your

game plan for three to five hours and then have the endurance to wake up and do it all over again the next day. In other words you have to be more then just a great ball striker these days; you have to also be a great athlete.

Believe this, too: Athletes aren't born, athletes are made. Oh sure, someone might have been blessed with outstanding physical traits but that by no means grants that person a free pass into athletics. You still must put in the practice time needed to develop your fundamental skills and that takes discipline.

To become a truly great athlete you must be disciplined. Every champion of every sport will tell you a story or two of the sacrifices they had to make and the discipline it took to succeed. You must be disciplined in order to develop the sound fundamentals of your desired sport if you want to be successful at it, because it will be those fundamentals that you are going to fall back on throughout your career when things go wrong or need fixing. The only way you will have sound fundamentals is if you have the discipline to practice them regularly.

There was a time when a tennis professional only needed to be skilled in the five fundamental tennis strokes to be successful, but not any-more. Now you must not only be a skilled ball striker but also have the ath-letic qualities of various other sports such as: the endurance of a marathon runner, the speed of an Olympic sprinter, the agility of a wrestler, the quickness and leaping ability of a basketball player, the hand eye coordi-nation of a baseball player and the mental toughness of a golfer.

A professional tennis player today goes through a long layer build-ing development process to reach that point where he or she is ripe, ready to be picked and shipped off to the market of professional tennis. That process takes time and there are no shortcuts. Let me say that again, there are no shortcuts. You build layers onto yourself, as a player each and every time you work hard in a practice or grind out a tough match and no one should be sent into the market of professional tennis until those layers are laid thick and the time is right. The game is too demanding to go in unpre-pared. It has changed immensely, that you already know, but what you might not know is that it is still constantly changing. If you don't change along with it you will get passed by every six months or so.

In the 80's and through the 90's it was the tennis academies that were thought to be a surefire path to the market of professional tennis. Kids from ages 3 to 18 were hitting thousands of balls daily in tennis factory type environments that had the resources but forgot to consider two very important key ingredients for success: one, individualism and two, fun. The academies will always be around so let's forget about them for a moment. The great players of today and those of tomorrow have succeeded and will succeed by putting layers upon layers of private, isolated practices on their games. That means home schooling if you're still a junior player and it means getting the right coach that you feel comfortable with and who has your best interests at heart. That way your own creative style, and mental approach to your game can be developed without distractions, all while still having fun. Just ask the two best players I ever coached, Venus and Serena Williams, how that worked for them. I do know they had fun.

As a player you can't afford to not have fun playing the game. This is a big ingredient in any kind of success you want to have in your life but especially in your tennis life. If you look back at why you started playing in the first place I'm sure you'll see it was because you enjoyed being outside on the tennis court slugging balls as hard as you could across the net or just because of the great exercise it provided you. I truly don't think any player can ever reach his or her full potential if they don't really love playing the game. It makes you want to chase down that extra ball at break point or go for that unbelievable drop shot at deuce or dig out an opponents deep ball at set point.

The bottom line is if you love what you're doing you'll never have a problem getting the most out of you. The toughest competitors tennis has ever seen were those that truly enjoyed the game, and it showed. Players like Connors, Courier, Seles and Graf showed how much they truly loved to play this game through their efforts on the courts each and every day of their careers.

If you are a coach or parent reading this, that ingredient of fun is something not to be forgotten. With the incredible amount of money that is now available in the game it is important that you don't get blinded by the lure of fame and fortune if you want your player to have a long and successful career. Burn out is always a possibility when too much pressure is applied. Sure, professional tennis is also a business and you have to take that business-like attitude in many decisions you make along the way, but

you just can't afford to make that decision constantly first when it comes to your player if you want them to grow inwardly as well as outwardly.

You also can't afford to follow old directions or read tennis books written ten and twenty years ago because this game, the New Game, only moves one way and that way is forward. By the time you read this book something may already be outdated. This book is aimed toward original thinkers; forward thinkers, those who want to add their names to this ever-changing new breed of players who will usher the game into the future. But if you don't fall into this category and only wish to improve on your game at a social level then there's plenty of helpful advice in here for you too.

Remember this is a sport that has a continuous ladder of skill levels and knows no age limitations. Just take a trip to the local public courts and you'll see players from eight to eighty battling it out in a three set match. And that's what I love about this sport, no matter what age you are, as long as you can serve and keep score then you can be on the court playing. Unlike the numerous computer games of today that do nothing for you but entertain your eyes and stimulate a few brain cells, when you're playing a tennis match, your learning more then just how to keep the ball inside the lines, you're learning a lot about yourself. How? By being out there on the court on your own, making countless important decisions under pressure, all of which affect an outcome. The experience of those decisions that you layer upon yourself is something that builds self-confidence and can be used in every other aspect of your life. As you start making better decisions on the tennis court you may find you'll start making better decisions in your life as well. Enough said, let's get on with turning you into a tennis player athlete of the New Game.

The Five Tennis Fundamentals

There are five basic fundamental ingredients that I've found which are essential in becoming a high-level tennis player athlete. I base my entire coaching methods around these five fundamentals and this book will repeat them over and over again in each chapter but in this chapter let's define each one and then talk about two that can take you the highest on the world tennis ladder. The five fundamentals are:

1.   **Early preparation**
2.   **Footwork**
3.   **Staying down**
4.   **Racquet Speed**
5.   **Mental Game Skills**

When things go wrong with your game, these are the basic fundamentals you will need to go back to when retooling. You've heard of the K.I.S.S. rule. It's been taught to all of us in some area of life and still stands true today; **keep it Simple Stupid**. It's great to have a million different spins or ways to hit a ball but too many choices can sometimes cause confusion, which can then bring about frustration. When your game is on and your opponent's is not, go right ahead and try new things; venture outside your comfort realm and experiment. That's how you get better, that's how you grow as a player. But when your opponents game is on and giving you fits what do you do then? Keep it simple and go back to your fundamentals. Think, stay down better, move your feet faster, get your racquet back sooner, maintain racquet speed and get tougher. When you get back to the fundamentals you'll be able to problem solve much better. You'll then find out which fundamentals were lacking in your defense of your opponents offense. If there's still time, and in tennis there always is, then you can turn the match around and be the one on top in the end.

This back to the fundamentals approach can be applied to all areas of your game as well as all areas of your life. As a student in mathematics,

when I was stuck on a problem, I can't tell you how many times my teacher would prescribe that I go back to the root of the problem and start again. Going back never seemed right to me but in the end I always was able to work out the problem. In English class, when diagramming sentences, you are taught to find the fundamentals first: noun, verb and adjective. Without these fundamentals you can't figure out the more difficult parts of the sentence structure and you fail to dissect the problem. Having good fundamentals doesn't always guarantee perfect play but it does help put the odds in your favor to have a good performance and to avoid that word that every athlete of any sport hates to hear, failure.

Early Preparation

When it comes to tennis fundamentals this is probably the first thing you were ever taught or ever heard from that person who threw you your first tennis ball to hit and it needs to be the first thing you still do when you see the ball coming to your side of the net. Remember these words, "OK now get your racquet back first."

Early preparation starts before your opponent hits the ball. It begins as you look across the net at the ball you have just hit. That's how early you should start gathering as much information as possible in order to anticipate and prepare for your opponents return shot. It does you absolutely no good to be fast to the ball if when you get there you are not positioned or prepared correctly for the type of ball hit by your opponent. It also does you no good even if you have analyzed your opponents shot type if you have not properly prepared the racquet to swing once the ball bounces. You might think this is very basic, and it is, but that's what fundamentals are, the basics of your game. Do them well and good things will come from them but do them poorly and you will often fail in achieving a high performance.

If you are a junior player who is in the developing stages of your game this is the time to start good habits. Having your racquet prepared, your wrists loaded and your feet in the proper position before the ball gets to you will easily save you twenty shots per set. That means you have the chance to win twenty points that you would have been out of if you hadn't

prepared early. I see too many junior players waiting until the ball is almost upon them before preparing and then there is no time for the decision making process in their shot making and that leads to poor shot placement or errors.

Imagine you're about to take a history exam or a driving test. Wouldn't you prepare yourself by reading the material first on what happened or on how to drive so that you could give yourself the best possible chance of succeeding? Of course you would. Getting prepared is a part of everyday life.

Stay Down

Staying down is the necessary first stage of putting power into your strokes and shots. In other words, if you want to hit the ball hard this is the key ingredient. And if you want to handle your opponents' hard hit shots this is also the key ingredient. I see too many players of all levels lose power in their shots or don't have the strength to handle opponents shots all because they have a bad habit, or an unwillingness or a laziness not to stay down. Standing up during your shot only loses power, which results in either a short ball, a ball in the net or the loss of control of the opponents shot. You must stay grounded completely through the contact zone if you want to be a powerful ball striker. Those of you who like to twirl out of your shot know this: you are breaking the kinetic chain by losing contact with the ground and you will often see your balls fly wildly beyond the baseline or come up short in the court. If you want to jump or lunge into a shot, which I recommend whenever possible, then you must first get low enough so that the energy stored in your preparation can be timed and released from the ground up and through the shot. If you miss calculate the timing of the shot and jump too early then you'll be in the air with nothing more then your upper body power to hit the shot. If you stay down and time the jump or lunge properly though you'll then have both the power from the ground and the uncoiling power from your upper body into your shot.

If you're not sure how low you need to be, I suggest you go to the local basketball court in your neighborhood or a nearby gym and play some one-on-one with a friend or a coach. When you're on the defense try guarding your friend by standing straight up in your legs and in your back. I bet you'll see your friend drive around you all day long for easy lay ups. Now try getting down low in a defensive position with your knees bent, your stance wide and your back straight and notice how you will have stopped your friend's drive to the basket. That's how low you'll need your stance to be on the tennis court. I like the use of other sports in your cross training of your tennis skills and basketball is one sport that has similar footwork, stance and cardio needed in tennis. More on cross training for tennis in the Futuremetrics chapter.

Footwork

Being fast to the ball and quick around the court is a fundamental that can be the biggest advantage to any player caught in a battle with an opponent of equal ball striking skills. It's also a fundamental that I feel can always be improved upon no matter what level of this game you are currently playing at.

I've had some players in the past that believed, when they first came to train with me, that speed and quickness were gifts that only other players had, and that they were just not as gifted in that part of the game. But after hours upon hours of footwork drilling they came to know better! Footwork can be practiced and improved upon just like any other tennis fundamental and, as you'll read in further detail later, I believe that footwork is one of only two areas of your game, that if practiced regularly, where you can forever gain a big advantage on the rest of the players in your class.

Improving your footwork should be included in your goal setting at the beginning of the year along with the tournaments you want to win and the strokes and shots you want to own. And be specific in what it is you want to improve upon. Maybe it's a better first step or a quicker sprint that you want or possible it's a quicker recovery step or a better or more frequent split step. Whatever it is you may lack in your footwork skills it can always be improved upon and it should be a constant goal in your tennis-playing career.

Racquet Speed

This fundamental is so important for your serves, baseline, mid-court and most all your shots that without it your game will be like an error bomb waiting to explode every match. No matter what type of ball your opponent hits at you it is important that you have the proper wrist snap generating racquet head speed to counter the speed and spin of their shot, and to do that it means you'll need strength.

Your stroke is sure to break down during a match if you are not strong enough to maintain your racquet speed throughout a three set or five set match. Your opponent's ball will constantly feel heavy on your strings if you can't or haven't generated any racquet speed at contact time. Unless you are hitting a shot with neutralizing or pace changing qualities then you should always be accelerating through the ball. Players' who try to place a shot into an open court by decelerating thinking they have better control if they slow down their swing, know this; in the New Game players are just too fast and their shots too powerful that any deceleration or poorly struck ball into an open court will easily come back to you with power. In other words, if you are not taking it to your opponent then they are going to take it to you. If you are a junior player and still playing high looping style shots with deceleration in any of your writs snaps, then you need to start changing your ways now because that game style will not get you out of junior level tennis. Even if you are currently having success, you need to try to start taking balls on the rise and maximizing your racquet speed at all times.

So how do you get racquet speed? It's all in how you time your shots so that the energy you load during the preparation phase of your swing is released through the uncoiling of your hips and shoulders and the snapping motion of your forearm and wrists at contact time that determines your racquet speed. Upper body strength, which includes: abdominal, shoulder, forearm and wrists, becomes very important in maximizing racquet speed while leg strength is important in order to keep you balanced and grounded so that the upper body can uncoil and release into the shot. If you haven't already started one, then you should have a strength program incorporated into your overall tennis training. Your strokes and shots are sure to reward you with increased power and spin if you have the necessary strength to maintain racquet speed. Besides this game is more fun if you can, grip it and rip it!

Mental Game Skills

If you have become a skilled ball striker that has learned to stay down and work your feet then the only fundamental left to help decide the outcome of your match is what's inside you. Your mental game. Being skilled mentally is the second area of your game where, I believe, you can forever gain a big advantage on everyone else in your class. I will go into further detail below, but the bottom line is that to be able to stick to your game plan, perform tactically under pressure and think yourself out of tough situations is what having a mental game and being mentally tough is all about.

I was at a junior tournament once in Kansas City watching some of the new talented 14 and under hopefuls play through the first three rounds of a designated tournament. After watching a number of the talented ball strikers, one not so talented caught my attention more then the rest. Her strokes were unorthodox but her footwork; use of tactical plays and her desire to chase down every ball was winning her matches. She had frustrated her opponents into self destructing through her first three rounds and the morning before her fourth round I saw her in the field next to the tennis center sprinting and jumping rope an hour before her match time, a routine she had done before each of her previous matches. Because she was not a seeded player or one of the current players in the USTA system, she was not getting any attention by the local media covering the event. Her next opponent was the number two seed who had beautiful strokes and hit powerful shots. She showed up about twenty minutes before the match and used that time to have a nice breakfast and chat with the other top players playing that particular morning.

As I stood by the court observing the pre-match warm up a local reporter came up to me and began conversation.

"This should be a quick match for the seed wouldn't you say coach?"

"Truly, I think the seed has her hands full today," I said.

"Are you kidding me," he asked?

"No I'm quite serious," I said.

"Coach, that girl," he said pointing to the seed's opponent, "is unseeded and just look at those strokes. Even I know bad technique when I see it. She doesn't stand a chance."

"Sure her groundstrokes are unorthodox, her volley doesn't have any stick to it and her serve lacks power but she'll most likely win this match."

"Can I quote you," he asked with a slight chuckle to his voice.

"Sure," I said.

"Then I'll see you after the match," he said and then he walked away.

It was a close first set but after losing a 5-3 lead and then the set, the seeded player self- destructed and lost the match in straight sets.

The reporter I had talked with earlier came over after the match with a grin across his face, "Ok coach what did I miss," he asked?

"You forgot to factor in the fact that, in some cases, what's on the inside of a person matters more then what you see on the outside," I said.

He nodded his approval and then rushed away to go get a quote from the winning girl.

It was a good lesson for the seed that had obviously taken the match lightly in her preparations of her opponent with the unorthodox strokes. A lesson, whether learned or not I'll never know, on how to win with good footwork and mental toughness. The two fundamentals that I believe can give you the edge at any level.

Two fundamentals that can give you the Edge

As I mentioned, there are two fundamentals that can continuously give you the edge in your matches and that can always be improved upon no matter what level you are playing at. They are your footwork skills and your mental game skills.

If you've watched a Professional tennis tournament either on TV or live, you may have noticed that all the players seem to hit every shot well, all the players have pretty good serves and all the players can volley. So what is it then that is separating all the good players from the great players? Again it's their footwork skills and their mental game skills. Let's talk about the footwork first as without it you'll never have a chance to exercise the mental aspect of the game anyway.

Let's go back to that tennis match you're watching. Now stop watching the ball go back and forth over the net and instead just watch the feet of one of the players. Notice what they do with their feet right before their opponent hits a shot. Notice what they do before and after they hit a shot. That's footwork. Those splits, sprints, shuffles and recovery steps that you see happen are the key footwork fundamentals that separate the Venus Williams' and the Leyton Hewitt's from everyone else.

Once you reach a high level of play you'll notice that your opponent on the other side of the net equally matches your bigtime forehand or your sizzling serve. So how are you now to gain that advantage that you always had over lesser players with your big shots? The answer is footwork, footwork and more footwork. Here are the basic footwork techniques that you will need to become skilled at in order to get that edge.

The Split Step

The split step will be the most used form of footwork in your game. It happens every time your opponent is about to hit a shot no matter where you are standing on the court. Before you go sprinting for a ball you must get some sense of balance and shift your weight to your toes so that you are ready to spring to the ball. The split step does that for you. Before you turn to hit a groundstroke you need to get your legs up under you for power, the split step does that for you. Before you hit a volley you must stop your forward momentum so that you can then move in any direction, again it is the split step. The following photos show the progression of the split step.

| split step beginning | split step in the air | split step finish |

The split step is a small hop that splits your feet apart just beyond shoulder width. You should try to time your split steps so that your toes touch the ground just as your opponent is striking the ball that way you will be ready to spring in any direction. Land with your knees slightly bent and your weight forward on your toes so that you're ready to do the next footwork skill, the sprint.

Sprints

Learning to sprint to a ball and not just run, jog or walk, is something that you hopefully learned at a young age. But if not, you can still do it and improve upon it. If you need to get from sideline to sideline why not get there as fast as you can? I've seen a lot of amateur players, over the years that had beautiful groundstrokes as long as they didn't have to sprint. But once they had to sprint to get into position to hit a ball, then their shots and strokes would crumble like three-week old cookies. Mainly because they would try to time their steps perfectly with the oncoming ball instead of sprinting into the proper position, as fast as they could, so that they could then get their feet set to hit a balanced groundstroke. Sprinting into position is a key ingredient for increasing the power level of your shots because as you begin to set your feet quicker in your stance you will then be able to transfer your weight and uncoil your stored energy through the ball, from the ground up.

To be a good sprinter means that you can reach your maximum velocity by optimizing the relationship between your stride length and your stride frequency. The variables that make that happen are: leg strength, overall muscle strength, flexibility, muscle power (which is strength and speed combined) and quickness of reflexes. To check your sprinting ability, put yourself through the following top five sprinter's test: (you will need a stopwatch and a measuring tape—goals are listed)

Top Five Sprinter's Test

1. **From a sideline, take ten strides. How far did you go? (12-20 yards)**
2. **Do a long jump from a standing still position. How far did your heels go? (2-4 yards)**
3. **Measure 30 yards and take a running start and time the run at maximum velocity. (Try and get under 4 seconds)**
4. **Measure 30 yards and from a standing still position time acceleration run. (Under 4.80)**
5. **Find out how much weight you can half-squat. Now using half of the maximum half-squat weight, how many reps can you do in twenty-five seconds?**

Once you have each of the times, distances and reps measured, work on improving in each area. Tennis players like sprinters, need strength and power in pushing off and when changing direction, strong abdominal muscles to stabilize the hips and strength and speed in the shoulders and arms.

Tennis at its highest level is full of players with Olympic-like speed to the ball so you better go to the courts or the track right now and work on

your sprints so you won't look like you're standing still in your next match. (For more on improving your sprinting ability see the Futuremetrics chapter)

The Recovery Steps

Once you've learned to get your balance with a split step and get into position with a sprint then you'll need the final footwork ingredients, the recovery steps.

Your ability to recover after retrieving a very wide or a very deep ball will often be the deciding factor in whether or not you'll ever beat a high caliber player like a nationally ranked junior, club champion or Pro. Why? Because when you consistently recover back into position, you are saying to your opponent, "Hit me another wide ball because I love to chase them down," or "Is that the best you've got, because I got that one easy?" That type of footwork, attitude and desire begins to wear on your opponent and can eventually break them down physically, because of the extra shots you'll make them play, or mentally, because the court will begin to seem small.

There are three types of recovery steps that you must be skilled at to get you back in position. The first is the Crossover Step, which is used after retrieving a very wide ball that takes you well outside the singles side-lines and out of position, leaving a large portion of open court behind you.

The Crossover Step is just as it says, a step of the outside foot crossing over the inside foot. The purpose is to make up as much ground as possible with that one step before you have to sprint or shuffle. In the photo sequence below notice the crossover move made with the outside foot just after hitting an open stance forehand. The last photo shows the shuffle step.

| open stance forehand stance | crossover recovery step | shuffle step |

The Side-Lunge Step is the second recovery step and it is used on balls that aren't as wide but still take you out of position leaving an area of court open that you must shut down quickly. The side-lunge is a quick lunge step of the inside foot that keeps your body squared to the net in case you have to move back in the direction from where you just came. In the photo sequence below see how the foot that is inside the court is lunging back to begin the recovery process, followed by the shuffle step.

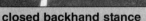

| closed backhand stance | side lunge recovery step | ready position stance |

The Shuffle Step

The shuffle step is what is used right after both the crossover step and the side lunge step (shown in the last pictures of both the above photo sequences) to aid in your recovery. It is the quickest way to move around the court in short distances of 5-10 feet to either side. The shuffle step is performed by keeping your shoulders and hips squared to the net with your knees bent while moving quickly to the side and without crossing your feet over one another. This is the same footwork a basketball player uses while playing tight man-to-man defense and it should be your primary movement in your recovery defense.

I cannot stress enough how important I believe footwork to be in your game. Coaches and parents of young players do your player a huge favor and start them on a footwork program now. They'll thank you later when they can move around the court like a cat retrieving balls that were once thought to be untouchable.

Top-five Drills for Great Footwork

1. The Georgia Star Drill—Improves sprinting, leg strength and change of direction.

2. Suicide Shuffles—Improves a player's lateral movement and ability to stay down.

3. Hillside Sprints—Find a steep hill, a bridge or football stadium bleachers and practice-timed sprints to the top. Improves speed and endurance.

4. Two Ball Pick-ups—Improves lateral and forward quickness as well as strength.

5. Jump rope—This could be the easiest and fastest way to better your footwork and it only takes 10 minutes a day. Do 1 minute on each foot, then 1 minute both feet, then 2 minutes alternating feet, then do 1 minute high jumping where your knees go to your chest, then do 2 minutes skipping across the court, then do 1 minute jogging in place and finally 1 minute of two stepping between each jump.

(See Drill pages in back for explanation of Footwork drills: 1, 2 & 4)

Michael Chang

In professional men's tennis, there have always been guys who were fast to the ball and quick around the court. But if you ask ten people who was the fastest or the quickest, eight out of ten would probably say Michael Chang.

Michael Chang's footwork around the court was without a doubt his biggest weapon. And in a game full of powerful forehands and big serves he used his weapon to not only neutralize opponents but also frustrate them into self-destructing. He was probably the best number two player in the world without a big serve or dominate groundstroke. He had the heart of a lion though and the speed and quickness of a panther and using those attributes he chased down balls that even the spectators watching had at times given up on. Just imagine how frustrated Chang's opponents used to get watching their very best shots come back over the net with no point won or no advantage gained. All because of his great footwork around the court.

So next time you're in a tough match against a worthy opponent, give yourself the edge and the best possible chance at winning by moving quickly around the court and trying to be, as they say, like Mike.

The Mental Game Skills

How you see your game, how you analyze your opponent's game and how you approach different points, games and match situations is what makes up your mental game skills and what is many times the key fundamental that separates you from losing or winning. The good thing is that the mental game can be practiced and developed just like any of the other tennis fundamentals.

I've heard many times people refer to certain players as not being mentally tough. Believe me that is not a phrase that you ever want to be label with, and it doesn't have to be. If you practice your mental skills regularly then you will get mentally tougher. Certain mental skills of the inner you like focus, self-discipline, attitude and confidence can be practiced off the court as well as on, while other mental skills get developed only through match play. Like when you dig deep and comeback in a match that your down in or when you out perform your opponent in pressure point, game and match situations. Excelling in those situations adds needed mental toughness layers to your game and on the pro tour it's those layers of mental toughness that are a key ingredient found consistently in every Grand Slam champion and every former number one player of this game.

Develop The Inner You

To truly develop strong mental skills I believe you have to spend some time alone inside yourself. Why? For the simple reason that there won't be any one else on the court with you to help you when you're facing break points or when you've just lost the first set. No, the only ones on that court who can help you get through the tough points, games and sets is you, and the inner you. Whose the inner you?

Haven't you been in a tough match and heard that little voice inside your head? You know, that little voice that you constantly have dialog with during your matches. That voice that sometimes helps you believe that you can do it but also sometimes tries to get you to give in and say that you can't. That voice you hear is your inner you.

Still don't know who or what voice am I talking about? Think back to when you first learned to swim. When your skills got good enough to swim the width of the pool the challenge then became the length of the pool. As you sat there looking to the other end of the pool that voice inside you may have said, "Go for it! You can swim far now." If you believed in yourself then there was probably not much more dialog but if you didn't believe you were ready for such a task then the inner you may have talked yourself out of the challenge and waited until another day. That inner you dialog is a part of your mental game at work. Still not sure what or who I'm talking about?

How about when you first were learning to ride a bike? Probably every time you crashed your mother or father or who ever was teaching you picked you up off the ground and said to get back on and try again. But before you got back on that bike seat I bet your inner you had something to say. If you did get back on then your inner you was positive and even if you crashed again you took one step forward towards developing your mental toughness but if you gave up then your inner you must have been negative and your mental development was slowed.

Your goal is to develop a positive inner you and leave out all the negative self-doubt. Easier said then done, sure, but know this: those players who mope around the court in a negative way constantly belittling themselves, their opponents or the umpires, are the easiest to defeat. Why? Because they haven't developed a confident positive mental approach to their game. They let everyone and everything around them get inside their head and interfere with that inner voice dialog that should only be going on between them and their inner selves.

As a high level player you just can't afford to have any self-doubt about your game at all. If you truly don't believe you can beat Venus Williams before you step on the court to play her then you can't and you probably never will. But if you believe in yourself and in your game and your approach to your game is a positive one then you definitely have a chance. When it comes down to beating or becoming a champion, it really is what's inside you that counts most.

Like I said before, if you want to develop a strong mental game then you need to spend some time alone. Here are some ways you can work on your mental game skills to help you play tougher tennis and develop a strong and positive inner you.

Top Five Mental Game Drills

1.Self Service—Go to the tennis court by yourself to work on your serve. Don't take a friend, a coach or a family member with you, just you and a basket of balls. Play out pressure point and game situations in your head using the placement and spin of your serve to determine whether or not you win or lose the points. For example pretend the score is 15-40 and your opponent has a weak backhand. Serve yourself out of trouble by placing all your serves into the backhand corners with slice until the game is over. Now don't let yourself off the hook by giving yourself the point on a ball that doesn't hit the backhand corner or goes in flat instead of with spin. Do this situation until you can repeatedly win every game and then change the serve placement and the spin. Spend at least one hour on the court by yourself every other day until you own your serves. Don't forget to play against both right-handers and left-handers.

2. Visualization—This is an increasingly popular technique performed by top athletes of most sports. This again involves the need for you to be alone by yourself, preferably in a relaxing atmosphere. Imagine yourself performing certain parts of your game in a positive way. For example suppose your forehand and kick serve have been unreliable lately and you just can't seem to beat a serve and volley style player. Try fixing the problem mentally by imagining yourself hitting repeatedly perfect forehands and perfect kick serves in a match against a serve and volley style player. See yourself hitting forehand passing shots as the serve and volleyer rushes the net. Watch as your kick serves bounce over the returnee's head. It's OK to imagine great and wonderful shots like a kick serve bouncing over the back fence. Just try to keep all your thoughts and imageries positive.

Try visualization five to ten minutes everyday just before practice. For example If you have been having trouble keeping your shots inside the lines, then imagine yourself hitting all your shots so that they always land exactly two feet from any line. Do this just before your practices or matches and I think you'll notice a positive increase in your performance.

3. Hocus Focus—If your concentration or focus is weak during your matches try this technique. Before your next practice session try starring at a tennis ball for five minutes just before stepping on the court. Notice the seams, the color, the felt and the lettering on the ball. Now when you begin hitting try to hit the seams or the letters while noticing the color and felt changes as the ball gets hit back and forth across the net. In other words, focus only on the ball. See how long you can go before your concentration is broken and you begin looking at something else. Was it 10 minutes, 5 minutes or 1 minute? Work on improving that time. In a match see if you can block out everything and focus solely on the ball.

4. Develop Winning routines—The great player knows that playing great tennis is not an accident; it is a series of well-executed actions performed within their game plan. Next time you find yourself hitting great serves in a practice or in a match take the time to notice exactly what you are doing. How are you stepping up to the line, how many times are you bouncing the ball on your first serves and on your second serves, what is your mind thinking just before delivering that ace and how much time are you taking in-between serves? You will probably find that your well-executed actions are routines that keep repeating. That's good! Now after that practice or match go write down exactly what routine you were doing that produced such good serves and practice repeating them. The same goes for every other stroke or shot, or shot combination, or mental approaches of your game. Always note what you were thinking of or focusing on during those days of great shot making or great match play. Also note what you did before you stepped on the court, what you ate and any other factors you can remember that may have aided you in your superior performance. Soon you will have your own written guide to follow on how to play great tennis every time you go to the courts.

5. Dump the Garbage—Winning tennis matches is all about staying mentally positive. No matter what negative things are going on in your match you have to be able to stay positive if you want to win. Try to get rid of the negative thoughts and feelings that arise throughout a match as soon as possible. To do that practice this technique: Since you have 20 seconds in between points use that time to walk to the back fence and *dump* all the negative thoughts, anxiousness, stress, self abuse, hopelessness, frustration, nervousness and anything else that is disrupting your play. Don't step up to serve or return serve until your mind is clear. Some players step off to the side and straighten their strings or towel off their grip when they need to focus. What's important is that you take the time to get rid of the negative garbage that can arise during a match and manifest itself into three point swings or even worse three game swings.

Next time you are practicing situations or playing a match and you have just played a poor point try taking a walk to the back fence to dump the garbage before playing that next point. You'll soon begin to stop those three point swings and become a much tougher point-to-point player.

❖ *The Venus & Serena Factor* ❖

If there's two areas of the women's game that have been effected most by Venus & Serena its, in being athletic on the court and for being mentally tough competitors, intimidating competitors.

In the seven years I spent with Venus & Serena I saw everyday their desire to win at all cost no matter if it was simply a drill game to eleven points, a practice match or a hitting challenge. They were out to win, succeed, achieve and they never believed they couldn't do it. Sure they were blessed with their athletic gifts but that didn't keep them from working hard everyday at being stronger or faster; instead they improved upon their gifts to become the best they could be.

One day, caught up in practice match battle, Venus ran down a fairly good drop shot of mine that had her sliding by the net post and near the court canopy where her mother was watching as she executed her shot. She was very excited to get my drop shot and said, "You know, there's not a single drop shot that I can't get," showing a little cockiness.

Her mother quickly responded by saying, "If you think you can get to any drop shot then you should be able to get to any ball."

Venus stood for a moment and looked at her mother, who hadn't

said a word all practice, and then took in her mother's advice. She then proceeded to chase down every one of my shots the rest of that day and even if she didn't execute the shot, she made sure the ball didn't bounce twice, which in turn added some speed and quickness to her movement and mental toughness to her game.

On the WTA tour today, all those who used to win with just great ball striking skills, know now, that if Venus & Serena are in the draw then they're in for an athletically fierce battle, full of long hard points and lots of intimidating shots.

Player Note:

Today's top players spend as much time off the court working on improving their mental game skills and athletic ability as they do on the court improving their tennis shot making and ball striking skills. Know this, you eventually will reach a ceiling to your tennis playing skills and the only way to raise that ceiling is by improving your athletic ability. This game is still about shot making don't get me wrong. And being a great shot maker will take you far but to compete at the highest level of the New Game you are going to have to be more then just a tennis player, you are going to have to be, a tennis player athlete.

Coach's Notebook

Early Ages (5-9)—Practice the fundamentals over and over again! Don't start trying to learn the difficult touch shots or power shots until the fundamental base has been properly established. Correct grips should be introduced but not enforced at this time, not until the proper strength is developed. Be careful not to discourage creativity at this point just reaffirm the importance of the five key tennis fundamentals. Concentration and focus will be the first mental skills that need to be developed. Footwork drills can and should be a part of every practice. As a coach or parent, make sure the ingredient of fun is apparent in every practice and that you aren't forcing the game on your player or child. If they'd rather be doing something else, then let them. When they're eager to practice, then they'll practice harder, develop quicker and retain more.

JR Tournament Level Player—Practice everyday the five key tennis fundamentals as well as the fundamentals of each stroke and shot you've learned so far. When things go wrong with a certain shot or stroke, go back to your fundamentals to figure it out. You should be using all the correct grips at this point and if your not make the change today otherwise you'll get left behind. Begin to practice adding new shots into your game plan. Practicing footwork and mental game skills should be a part of your weekly on-court practice sessions as well as off-court training sessions. Those players that learn to control their anger; nerves, frustration and other emotions in junior competition will make a much easier and successful transition to pro-level tennis.

Pro-Level Player Beginnings —Now that you've become a skilled player it's important to become even more disciplined in your fundamentals. Keep looking for key areas in your game where you can make a fundamental better. Whether it's a faster way to get to a ball, an earlier preparation for a shot or a more balanced way of staying down to generate pace. If there's any weak fundamental in your game your opponents will find it at this level so it constantly needs attention. Your footwork and mental game skills are the two fundamentals where you will find you can continuously gain an advantage and should be an area of focus in each practice. During weeks with no tournament scheduled, focus on improving your footwork and playing against player styles that give you the most trouble. During tournament weeks, practice focus should be centered on shot making and tactics for upcoming opponents and fine-tuning of your mental game skills.

CHAPTER TWO

The Shots

There are a thousand different shots in this game and no two are exactly alike. I've always told my players to imagine that every ball that comes at you is like a snowflake, no two are exactly the same, and so you shouldn't treat them the same. But playing each ball slightly different means you'll need to develop the shot making skills to do so. You might know it in your head how you want to play a shot but you need to be able to feel it in your racquet. Even though you'll want to own as many shots as possible there are Twenty-Two shots that you need to own if you plan to play in the New Game at its highest level. Those Twenty-Two shots are:

RINEBERG

Twenty-Two Shots to Own

1. **Flat Serve**
2. **Slice Serve**
3. **Kick Serve**
4. **Topspin forehand**
5. **Slice Forehand**
6. **Inside-out forehand**
7. **Topspin Backhand**
8. **Slice Backhand**
9. **Forehand Volley**
10. **Forehand Swing Volley**
11. **Backhand Volley**
12. **Backhand swing volley**
13. **Forehand Smash**
14. **Backhand Smash**
15. **Forehand Drop Shot**
16. **Backhand Drop Shot**
17. **Forehand Return of Serve**
18. **Backhand Return of Serve**
19. **Backhand Lob**
20. **Forehand Lob**
21. **Forehand Approach Shot**
22. **Backhand Approach Shot**

So now that you know the shots just what does owning a shot mean?To own a shot simply means that you can hit that shot or some variation of that shot 90% of the time to specific areas of the court on any type of ball your opponent hits at you.

Take the Forehand Topspin groundstroke for example. If your coach or practice partner were to hit you ten shots to your forehand side all with different speeds and spins, you need to be able to hit nine of those ten with topspin to various areas of the court. If you can do that over and over again then it's safe to say that you **own** your topspin forehand shot. If your making too many errors though then you'll need to continue drilling it before stepping into any high-level competition, because if an opponent senses that you don't own that topspin forehand then he or she is going to pick on it the entire match. And if you yourself don't believe you own it then it won't take long before a few errors has you mentally psyched out to hit it.

You must own your shots! That's why tour players practice everyday. They know that match play is no time to be working out the problems of a stroke or shot they don't own and they know that any self-doubt about a stroke or shot during a match will only lead to defeat. Owning a stroke or shot gives you the confidence to use it under any pressure situation. That confidence then becomes a mental edge that will keep you focused on how to win the match rather then on what's going on with your strokes or shots during the match.

If you're already playing high-level tennis matches then you need to definitely spend time each practice on those shots and strokes that you still don't feel you own. It's important to set aside time but not to waste time as you want to continually add to and improve upon the game shots you already own.

Once every ten days or so I like to put my players through the following hitting test so that they can see as well as I can see which shots they own and which shots we need to continue to drill.

HITTING TEST 380(Approximate time 1hour)
Coach feeds from the center of the baseline to each specific shot zone.

20 balls to forehand – Player must hit topspin forehands to five areas of the court.
20 balls to backhand – Player must hit topspin backhands to five areas of court.
20 balls to forehand – Player must hit slice forehands to five areas of court.
20 balls to backhand – Player must hit slice backhands to five areas of court.
30 balls to forehand volley – Player must hit to seven areas including drop zones

30 balls to backhand volley – Player must hit to seven areas including drop zones.

10 balls to f-swing volley – Player must hit crosscourt and down the line.

10 balls to b-swing volley – Player must hit crosscourt and down the line.

20 Forehand smashes – Player must hit five areas of court

20 Backhand smashes – Player must hit five areas of the court.

20 f-drop shots – Player must hit two areas from baseline and mid court.

20 b-drop shots – Player must hit two areas from baseline and mid court.

20 Deuce court Returns – Player hits forehands and backhands to two zones.

20 Ad- court Returns – Player hits forehands and backhands to two zones.

20 Fh & Bkh-Approach shots – Player must hit two zones— down the line and crosscourt.

20 Fh & Bkh-lobs– Player must hit two zones—down the line and cross-court.

20 slice serves – Player must hit 3 areas in the deuce box and 3 in the ad box.

20 flat serves – Player must hit 3 areas in the deuce box and 3 in the ad box.

20 kick serves – Player must hit 3 areas in the deuce box and 3 in the ad box.

Coaches Note:

Change the parameters of the test each time by feeding the ball differently or from a different court location. For example: If you normally feed from the center of the baseline with a flat ball feed, try moving to a baseline corner and feeding a heavy topspin ball. The next test time move to the opposite corner and feed a slice ball and so on. Your job is to prepare your player for any type of opponent.

What if your player seems to hit all twenty-two shots great in practice but can't win a first round of a tournament? It might be because he or she is so used to the way you feed or hit the ball to them that they feel comfortable hitting all twenty-two shots. Well I suggest you don't let them get comfortable. Give them variety either in how you feed the ball or how you hit the ball. Bring in different hitting partners that hit differently and play different styles and don't forget to bring in the occasional lefty to really keep your player off balance. Soon you'll begin to see your player advancing out of first rounds and further in the draw. Other ways to change things up are to change the surface you are practicing on or change the intensity at which you practice.

Change the Surface

They say variety is the spice of life and a way to add variety to your game or your player's game is to change the surface. There are four surfaces that you will compete on if you reach the professional ranks. They are: clay, hard court, indoor carpet and grass. Each offers different offensive and defensive shot selections because of the way the ball's bounce is affected when making contact with the surface and although you need to be skilled in how to play on each surface you may find that your game really shines on one particular surface. That's fine as you're climbing the tennis ladder but as you get closer to the top make sure you have made the necessary game changes to comfortably play on every surface. If there were one surface I wouldn't go over board on scheduling practice time trying to get use to, it would be grass. The tour only plays on it for one month out of the year. The other surfaces are offered at tournaments all over the world more frequently throughout the year. Let's take a look at what specific skills you will need to incorporate when switching to the different surface types.

Clay Courts

The ball bounces slow and erratically high on the clay surface and because of that combination you will find you have to work hard, long and patiently at winning points. This surface neutralizes the power players and gives the edge to the baseline grinders who are skilled shot makers and have good footwork. Spin is magnified by the soft gritty surface and hitting both topspin and slice are necessary tactics. Because you'll be on court much longer because the points are longer, your footwork and physical fitness become key ingredients to your success. This is the best surface to learn the game on in my opinion because every point you win you usually

have to earn. Players who grow up on clay are known for having consistent strokes and great tactical minds.

Hard Courts

The ball bounces high, true and fast on the hard courts and because of that combination you will find you have to work hard and fast on this surface to win points. This surface complements the power players like, serve and volleyers and aggressive baseliners, but it also gives the speedy player a fighting chance. Hard courts can vary in speed depending on the top surface coating and the rule to live by is the thinner and more worn the surface paint the faster the court and the lower the bounce. Player's who learn to take the ball on the rise and who aren't afraid to come to the net will have the most success on the hard court.

Indoor Carpet

The ball bounce on most synthetic surfaces is low, true and fast and because of that combination you will find you have to work hard at staying down and fast at getting in position. Because you are indoors though you won't have the heat, wind and sun to factor into your game. This takes out the physical fitness edge that some players have and again gives the advantage to the more aggressive style power players. Indoor carpet is faster then most hard courts but still not as fast as grass. What's underneath the carpet usually determines how fast the court will be. Spin is rewarded on the indoor carpet. A good serve will take you far into an indoor carpet tournament.

Grass

The ball bounces low, fast and erratic and because of that combination you will find you have to work hard at staying down and fast at reacting to the skidding bounce. The grass is a surface like no other and although it complements the power and spin in your shot it also can take power away or provide no bounce at all if there are dead spots. Because the grass surface is so slick the speedy player can often find himself or herself watching their opponents shot pass them by while sitting on the grass after trying to change directions too quickly. For that reason the edge goes to those serve and volleyers who only move in one direction, forward.

The Court Adjuster

Some of you might not have the luxury of having all four surfaces at your disposal to mix up practices. I faced that same issue in 1995 with two of my top players and that's when I came up with the idea of the court adjuster.

The most difficult adjustment to make when changing surfaces is in the timing of the return of serve. Because of that fact I decided to change the surface of our practice court's service boxes to mimic different tournament surfaces. We were already practicing on clay so all I needed to do was get a faster surface. I measured out the area of the service box and then went hunting for materials to make that part of our practice court faster. What I returned with was a roll of indoor/outdoor synthetic carpet and a sheet of linoleum. I glued the carpet to the backside of the linoleum and then painted the service box lines around the edges of each side so that whatever side I had it flipped to it would cover the service box perfectly.

The indoor/outdoor carpet side made the ball bounce low and fast much like an indoor synthetic surface or a perfect playing grass court. The linoleum side was lightning fast. In fact the ball bounce was so fast and low that it made a Wimbledon bounce look like it was in slow motion.

Our practices really got fun and after about two weeks my players began to get very good at returning serves off either side of the court adjuster. We even moved the court adjusters out of the service boxes and near the baseline to practice hitting groundstrokes off the faster surfaces. To stick to my plan of offering my players plenty of variety, I experimented with court adjusters that had thick shag carpeted sides to imitate slower surfaces and harder slick plastic sides to speed things up even more. For the rest of that year I could be seen driving around town with big roles of carpet sticking out of the passenger seat of my little red convertible.

Change the Intensity

The next thing you need to change in your stroke and shot making practices, to secure the fact that you do own them, is the intensity. When you as a player feel that the drill is becoming to easy or as a coach you see that what used to give your player a good work out now is routine, then it's time to up the intensity. How? By allowing less time between ball feeds or adding a stronger hitting partner to the practice sessions or by adding in two on one hitting drills or my favorite intensity change is to throw in some interval hitting drills.

Interval hitting drills are high intensity all court, all stroke, shot making drills that have a player performing at their maximum heart rate for a specified number of shots with timed rest, all within a specific timed set. For example this is an all-court interval drill sheet:
(Go through each column of 10 before proceeding to the next column.)

Round 1	Round 2	Round 3	Round 4	Round 5
	Ball Feed/Rest			
2/15	7/15	8/15	3/8	7/15
6/15	2/20	8/15	3/8	5/15
3/15	2/15	8/15	3/8	1/10
10/15	16/20	8/15	3/8	10/20
8/15	4/10	8/15	3/15	16/20
2/10	6/10	8/10	3/15	3/15
7/10	1/10	8/10	3/15	2/10
15/10	12/15	8/10	3/15	7/10
4/10	9/15	8/5	3/5	20/5
3/90	3/90	8/90	3/90	4/Stop

Note: You may find that a shot or stroke that you thought you owned begins to break down under the new interval time demands. If so, this is a surefire sign that something is weak or lacking in one of the following three key ingredients of your overall tennis athletic skills: footwork, strength or endurance.

Top Five Fundamental Strokes You Must Own

If you're just starting out on your climb to the top know this; all the shots you will learn to create are adapted from these five fundamental strokes.

1.	**The Serve**
2.	**The Forehand Groundstroke**
3.	**The Backhand Groundstroke**
4.	**The Forehand Volley**
5.	**The Backhand Volley**

These five strokes are the fundamental strokes of your game and are a must that you own at least one variation of each before you go experimenting on different shots, different surfaces and against different playing styles. For example a typical stroke variation to own might be: a topspin forehand, a slice backhand, a slice serve, a swing forehand volley and a slice backhand volley. Once you own at least one variation of each stroke start adding the other shots to your list.

The twenty-two shots mentioned earlier that are needed to compete at the highest level of the New Game are all variations of these five strokes. Many coaches like to categorize certain shots like: drop shots, lobs, overheads and swing volleys as specialty shots but there's nothing special about them. The drop shot is just an exaggerated slice volley motion, the lob is simply a half of a groundstroke swing, the overhead smash is just like a serve and swing volleys are simply topspin groundstrokes hit out of the air with maximum racquet speed.

Don't scare yourself out of owning these shots by putting them in a special category. And don't be fooled into thinking these shots should only be hit five percent of the time like I've heard some coaches say. If you own the shot, then use it. What's important is that you feel comfortable using it at anytime during a match no matter the situation.

If You Don't Own It, Practice it!

Don't hit any shot you don't own when in a tough match. Save that for the practice courts. I believe that if you play a shot that you don't own in a tight match situation then you are giving in, breaking down or worse, choking. For example if it's 4-4 and break point against you; don't try to hit a sidespin drop shot down the line if you haven't the shot in the first place. Let me say it again, save practicing that shot and all shots you don't own for the practice courts. I do advise however, that if your way ahead and in control of a match that you do begin incorporating a new shot or two that's in development, so that it can become a part of your overall game plan. Once you see the effectiveness of the new shot in a match you will gain the confidence in it to use it more often.

So what are you waiting for, get out to the practice courts and start putting in the hours needed to own your strokes and shots and soon you'll be more then just a one-shot-wonder, soon you'll be a twenty-two shot gunslinger!

❖ *The Venus & Serena Factor* ❖

Even though Venus was older, Serena was the one who owned the twenty-two shots first.

When Venus joined the tour she made her mark more with her power and athleticism then with her shot making. In fact all of her early losses in her career were to players who owned more shots and used different shots in their defense of Venus' power. The scouting report on Venus read that if you could stay in the rally for 3 or more shots then you had a chance and if you mixed up the pace and placement of your shots then Venus was error prone.

Serena however always practiced and played differently because she didn't own the power that Venus had until much later in her career. So she had to develop better angels, drop shots, lobs, deep topspins and every other shot in order to win her matches. When the power finally did develop into her game then she became unstoppable as we all witnessed in 2001-2003. The scouting report on Serena, even early on, read that she had more shots then Venus and that she was a mentally tougher competitor.

Coach's Notebook

Early Ages (5-9)—Begin with the development of the five fundamental strokes. Learn one variation of each stroke so that you can begin playing points with your coach in your practices. The sooner you can have practices that mimic actual playing conditions the sooner you can begin practicing situations. Begin working on owning the twenty-two shots, as it will take many layers of practice to own all twenty-two. As your ball striking skills improve then try to add new shots into your overall game plan. Try to practice every six weeks or so on a different surface to add variety, fun and experience layers to your shot making skills. Keep working hard at improving the five tennis fundamentals!

Jr Tournament Level Player—You should have at least one variation of the five fundamental strokes that you feel comfortable using at any given time during a match. Now which shots don't you own? Better get to work on them! In your practices and practice matches try incorporating a new shot each week. If it only takes twenty-two weeks to own all the shots that would be great but plan on longer. Continue to polish the skills of the shots you already own. Each shot has its own fundamentals, which you will need to practice regularly. Take the 380-hitting test every four weeks to see what's missing in your arsenal. Be sure to play tournaments on different surface types when possible. Try to incorporate new shots into tournament matches that you are in control of. Every time you lose a match find out why. If it was because of a lack of shots in your tactics then keep adding new shots in your practicing. You still have a lot of layers you need to add to your game and the path to the pros you are on is full of many pitfalls so don't stop working hard now. Set new goals, make new plans and continue trying to achieve.

Pro Player Beginnings— If there is a shot from the list you don't own then you probably aren't winning many tournaments. Keep practicing and advancing your strokes and variations of strokes to combat the different playing styles you are now up against. Look for micro adjustments to polished strokes or shots like grip placement, grip pressure, stance, racquet speed or footwork. If there is a particular surface type that you're not winning on then try to practice more on that surface type as well as work on playing tactics for that surface type.

CHAPTER THREE

The Forehand

The Forehand has to be one of your weapons! Let me say that again. The Forehand has to be one of your weapons. Why? Because it's the side with more options. It's the side you do more things from as you're growing up and so it becomes the more dominate arm. And because this dominant arm is behind your body on the forehand side, as the ball approaches you have more time to react, which allows you to be more creative which gives you more options. And executing those options is what can make any stroke a weapon.

The forehand has certainly changed over the years, as have most strokes, to compete with the power that has come into the game through racquet technology and through strength training. The physical demands on players today are more intense and more challenging. If we could rewind time and take a look at the early players you would see a lot of them using continental grips, a straight back straight through swing motion and a closed stance. All that was fine then as the game was neither as powerful nor athletic as today's game. But if you tried to return the 100mph-140mph serve of today with that old style stroke, you'd be lucky to get the ball over the net and most likely you would have the racquet ripped from your hand. Today's players have evolved the forehand into a stroke that combines athleticism, strength and fine motor skills to produce a stroke that is capable of hitting winners from everywhere on the court. Try this recipe to turn your forehand into a devastating weapon!

The Grip

There are many great forehands in the game today all with slight style differences but at the same time all with similarities. Of these great forehands you will notice that the grip has moved from the old school continental grip on the handle and is now in an eastern grip or even more so in a semi-western grip most of the time with even an occasional move to a full western grip. Whatever feels most comfortable to you is what matters most and you shouldn't try a grip that doesn't fit your style. The grip you have today though might not be the grip you have five years from now so don't fall in love with it. Every pro makes slight modification to his or her grip over time or has developed a feel for a variety of grips. But if you haven't chosen a grip yet or are looking to make a major grip change then I recommend the semi-western grip or western grip.

To find these two grips you must first locate the 'V' of your hand made by the thumb and the index finger. Place that 'V' on the racquet handle with the edge of racquet facing towards you, and then rotate your hand to the right until the thumb is positioned across the top of the racquet handle. You are now in a semi-western grip if you are right handed. A little more of a move to the right and you are now in a western grip. If you are left-handed you will move your hand to the left instead of the right.

continental grip

semi-western grip

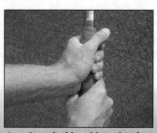
two handed backhand grip

The Swing

Once you have the grip it is important to use a back swing that compliments the grip while still feeling comfortable so that you can get the maximum power possible. The loop back swings, in three different forms, is my choice if you want to hit big time forehand*s* and you should be skilled in using all three variations.

Player Note: Keep in mind though, and this goes for all your strokes and shots, that it is not the backswing that hits the shot. All high level players know the importance of hitting through the ball with racquet speed and how their racquet goes through the contact point of the ball to the finish is what matters most when trying to execute a particular shot.

The Big C-loop, *the Little c-loop* and **the** *Hairpin-loop* are the perfect partners to the semi-western and western grips because of how they build momentum during the energy-loading phase of the swing and produce excellent racquet speed into the point of contact and on to the finishing phase of the swing.

To do these loop swings, pretend you are drawing the letter 'C' backwards in the air, if you're right handed. Raising your elbow to shoulder height during the backswing as the ball is approaching makes the **big C-loop** swing. If you keep your elbow down below your shoulder during the backswing you will make the **little c-loop** swing. In the photo sequence below you can see each stage of the **Big C-loop** swing.

| early preparation phase of the forehand | unloading phase of forehand | contact point of closed stance forehand | follow through of topspin forehand |

In the photo sequence below you'll notice that the **hairpin-loop** doesn't go as high as it does go back but it does round off in the backswing in the same way, as both the C-loops, to produce the same energy releasing racquet head speed through the contact point and on to finish.

Brittany hitting hairpin forehand loop

The Stance

The stance is the final ingredient to hitting big time forehands and it has also changed in the modern game. With players hitting so hard and accurate now a days there isn't a whole lot of time between shots to make your recovery. The open stance can save you four to six steps during a long baseline point and that means you can recover faster and keep the pressure on an opponent once an advantage has been gained. Because it is the outside foot that steps behind the path of the ball, in the open stance, it is not necessary to cross the inside foot over, as long as you have coiled your hips and shoulders properly. You will need to have good core strength to pull this off repeatedly. You still can't replace the closed stance for stability when driving the ball and for accuracy when hitting down the lines and I recommend that every player have the footwork to do either stance on any given shot.

open stance backhand   **open stance forehand**

Let's take a look at other key fundamental ingredients to the open stance forehand stroke in the photo sequence below. In the first photo notice how the left knee bends down and into the right leg as an open stance is taken. This is very important to properly insure that you are loading under the ball. Next the mid section (hips, stomach and trunk) begin to coil, which is where a player in the open stance stores power. The non-racquet arm is stretched out and does play a role. It keeps you the proper distance from the ball and provides balance right before you uncoil your body into the point of contact with the ball. From the low knee bent position in picture two, you can transfer your weight through your hips, rise up or even jump if you like, into the ball as your body completely uncoils releasing all stored energy. By being down and prepared early you are ready for the low skip bounce or even a bad bounce. As you've already learned, **Staying down is a key tennis fundamental!**

#1   #2

#3   #4   #5

In photo three as the weight is shifted from the back leg and the body uncoils into the point of contact, generating racquet speed through the ball becomes the most important concern. Racquet speed, that begins in the upper arm but is released only by properly snapping the forearm and wrist simultaneously through the point of contact. This simultaneous snapping of the forearm and wrist motion in the swing is, I believe, the key ingredient to generating maximum racquet speed.

Yes there is wrist snap in the modern forehand, lots of wrist snaps. Today's players must be able to do at least four different wrist snaps through the ball if they are to fire accelerating blows at times even when there is no time for much backswing. Those four wrist snaps are as follows:

The first wrist snap is used for high bouncing balls that get above your shoulders. You will want to loop your backswing as usual dropping the head of the racquet slightly below the ball but as you begin your upward attack on the ball take the racquet face across the backside of the ball and then down and across your backhand side so that the thumb of your racquet hand is pointed down upon completion. This snapping motion, also known as the windshield wiper swing because of how the racquet moves across the front of your body as a windshield wiper on a car windshield, is used to hit winners most successfully inside the baseline. To practice this try standing just inside the baseline and have a coach or practice partner hit high bouncing shots right at you. To drill this shot use the corner slap shot drill. (See drill pages)

The second wrist snap is used when taking balls on the rise below your shoulders around your waist. This is your driving zone and the area where you should look to hit your most penetrating shots. The swing is taken back in the same loop but instead of dropping below the ball you will want to cut the loop short and swing through on a flat plane to meet the rising ball. The wrist snap is timed with the rising ball so that the racquet face is flat at contact with the thumb pointing up. The wrist snap then goes out through the ball towards your desired target with a forward rolling snap motion that makes the palm of the racquet hand face the ground upon completion of the follow through. This is for added control to the flat stroke.

To drill this shot stand inside the baseline and have a coach or practice partner feed you topspin balls that rise into you on the bounce. For maximum power, time your shot so that the rising ball doesn't get above your chest.

The third wrist snap is used when taking balls that have completed their rise off the bounce and are now falling into the zone between your waist and your knees. This is your depth control zone where you have a little more time to choose whether or not to hit a deep drive, a placed set up

shot or a neutralizing shot by controlling the depth of your ball with a ball flight of moderate to excessive topspin.

The swing is looped back as usual but now must drop below the falling ball in time to snap the wrist up and through the back of the ball at contact as if you were trying to peel the cover off the ball with the racquet face. The thumb of the racquet hand is pointing down and away from the body at the contact point and then down and forward from the body upon completion of the follow through. If the follow through is completed correctly your palm of your racquet hand will be facing away from your body and your elbow will be pointing up.

To drill this shot, stand behind the baseline and have a coach or practice partner feed balls that bounce short and fall into you at about knee level. Practice placing this type of ball all around the court with concern on the ball's flight over the net.

The fourth wrist snap is used to counter an opponent's big shot that comes at you so fast that you have little or no time to prepare and are forced to just loop your wrist or just drop your wrist down in order to hit the shot back. Because of the pace of your opponents shot you will want to close your racquet face by facing the palm of your racquet hand slightly at the ground behind you and then using an abbreviated straight back straight through swing, snap straight through the ball as if you are trying to hit the ball into the top of the net. Don't try and lift the ball here, as this will send the ball too high over the net making for an easy put away or carry the ball too long. This half volley style stroke from the baseline can catch an opponent off guard and turn a defensive situation into an offensive one if the timing of the wrist snap is right.

To drill this shot stand on the baseline and have a coach or practice partner feed flat slap shots right at your feet. Practice the timing of the shot in relation to the shortened backswing.

Using these four wrist snaps with the loop styled swings will enable you to handle any type of ball that comes your way helping you to hit more, Big time Forehands!

Top-Five Drills for developing Big time Forehands:

1. High low Drill—Coach or practice partner hits high over the net with topspin while the player takes every ball on the rise and tries to hit flat and low over the net.

2. Hit Big or go Home Drill—Coach feeds soft shots all over court and player must swing away hitting forehands with maximum power.

3. Everything Inside-out Drill—Coach feeds to middle baseline and to backhand side and player must move around ball and hit all inside-out forehands.

4. Inside out——Not! Drill—Coach feeds balls to the middle of baseline and the player must move around the ball as if hitting an inside out shot but then hit instead topspin down the line.

5. The Corner Slap Drill—Coach feeds high mid-court feeds and player must hit slap shots to each corner.

(See drill pages for diagram explanations of each drill)

❖ *The Venus & Serena Factor* ❖

Venus Williams

From 1992-1999, I had the pleasure of working with one of the great tennis athletes of today's game, Ms Venus Williams. Some of you may think that because Venus is such a great athlete that she didn't have to work very hard on her strokes and shots, that it came easy to her. Well you are wrong. In fact, if not for a crucial grip change on her forehand in 1997, she may never have won her five Grand Slam singles titles and Olympic Gold medal.

It was two months before the 98 Australian Open a time of year that a lot of players who aren't in the top ten take off. But not Venus, not this particular year anyway. Although 1997 was a year full of firsts for Venus she wasn't satisfied. She had lost too often to the same players and many times it was her big forehand stroke that had let her down. She had always used an extreme western grip that was great for high bouncing

balls but the low driving balls that her opponents were hitting were caus-ing her to make a lot of errors, which in turn waned on her confidence. So she decided to make a major grip change to an eastern forehand grip, a grip that was more like her sister Serena's grip and a grip that would allow her to drive the ball more consistently.

Now with only two months to go before the next Grand Slam tour-nament most players wouldn't dare think of changing a grip; but Venus was determined to stop her losing ways. For the first three weeks of prac-tice in the new grip, there were a lot of shots that went over the back fence, bounced off light poles or ended up on the courtside awnings, everywhere but inside the lines. Most players would have given up on the idea at that point but not Venus. She was driven to become a Grand Slam champion and she knew she wouldn't get there unless she fixed the flaws in her game. So she stuck with it and a few weeks later it started to work. She began to handle low balls better and started making everything on the forehand side. The grip change had taken root and Venus was more consistent and more confident then ever.

It really was amazing to see Venus's willingness to change her pres-ent game so that she would be a better player in the future. A good lesson for any up and coming player. Besides the grip change, in that time I witnessed first hand that no matter how great of an athlete you are you still must have the drive and determination within, to become a champion.

Venus's new forehand settled comfortable into a semi-western grip and she made it to the Quarterfinals of that 98 Australian Open.

Coach's Notebook

Early Ages (5-9)—Begin with a straight back backswing for awhile, focusing mostly on **early preparation** and the contact point with the ball being out in front. As soon as there is enough strength start working on the loop swings. It's better to start in a closed stance until the legs and the core strength are stronger. Make sure balance and early footwork preparation are established. The western grip will feel the strongest to most players at this age but keep encouraging a slight move to the left for more of a semi-western grip. Start with a high topspin stroke that clears the net by at least a racquet length each time. Be careful not to start working on any wrist snaps until strong enough, as this can become an injury prone area of young players. Practice the fundamentals!

Jr Tournament Level Player—If you haven't already, get going on open stance forehands. Core strength should be a major concern in your off-court strength training. Make sure you have established an accelerated wrist snap through the point of contact and a follow through that has the elbow rotating up each time. Begin to work on the four wrist snaps needed to handle any ball. Begin to establish different ball flights to all areas of the court. Start establishing an inside-out forehand so that you can sit on the backhand side of the court and set up points to your forehand. Begin to establish different ball flights to all areas of the court by using different wrist snaps to change the degrees of spin on the ball. Learn to take away and add pace to any ball. Practice adding power to balls with no pace and neutralizing balls with pace. You should have the forehand side established as one of your weapons if not your biggest weapon.

Pro Player Beginnings—By now you should have established your forehand as a main groundstroke weapon. If you're already winning points powerfully off your forehand side then start using more angles, spins, drops and feel shots in practice to add variety. If you're already winning a lot of points with your variety then try to add more power. Are you ending points with your forehand? If not use shot combinations that entice opponents to hit more balls to your forehand side and make sure you have the footwork to run around any weak shot to the backhand side and hit forehands. Don't sit back and think you are done developing this stroke. Remember this game changes every time a new player enters at your level. You must be ready to handle that change.

CHAPTER FOUR

The Backhands

This chapter is titled **Backhands**, because in today's game you need more than one backhand stroke. One of the best player's I ever saw use two backhands so effectively was Mats Wilander. Oh sure other players had two backhands but usually only one was hit by choice and the other was hit in defense. But Wilander hit both his backhands offensively and by choice. He would drive the ball past his opponents using the power of his two handed topspin backhand or move them around the court and wear them down with the finesse and control of his one handed backhand slice. A perfect combination of both power and control and exactly my recipe for tennis players who want to play at the highest levels of the New Game.

The Two-Handed Topspin Backhand

I like the two-handed topspin backhand as the primary backhand because of the aggressiveness of the stroke but mainly for its offensiveness on return of serves. If you look at the best returners to ever play this game both men's and women's they have all been two-handed backhand players. It makes handling a powerful serve much easier and it gives you more angle ability when the wrist are snapped through the point of contact quickly. If your mobility is good and you have the power to be on the offense most of the time like a Monica Seles or an Andre Agassi then you can choose to use the two handed backhand 95 percent of the time.

Look to be aggressive and drive your two handed backhand flat to end points quickly when balanced and in position but also use your two handed topspin shot to create angles and keep the ball deep. If you can't angle your backhand or keep it deep then it won't matter how well you can drive it because everyone at the highest levels of the New Game can handle pace hit straight ahead. To hit the two handed backhand offensively try this recipe:

The Grip

To take a two-handed grip put the bottom dominant hand in a continental grip and the top non-dominant hand in an eastern to semi-western forehand grip. Keep the hands together leaving no space between them. Some players like to separate the hands for more stability but I feel it hinders the snap and the angle ability that you get with the hands together. Keep both hands loose until you start the backswing then try a move that I call *The Russian Twist*.

The Russian twist is performed when you squeeze and turn your grip from a forehand into a backhand on the handle of the racquet as if you were wringing out a wet towel. It happens as you move the grip of the lower dominate hand from a semi-western forehand to a continental grip and as your arms begin to extend behind you on the backhand side. This is the beginning phase of the swing when you begin coiling your shoulders, hips and torso into the energy-loading phase of the swing. It's not for everyone but *The Russian Twist* does help some players' load the wrists better to produce more wrists snap into and through the contact point.

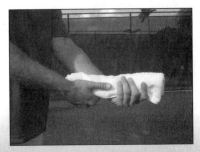

Russian twist towel grip

loading the Russian twist is like wringing out a towel

The Two-Handed Stance

You need both the open and closed stances. Use an open stance when moving wide and when returning most serves and use a closed stance when moving forward or driving the ball. Having the ability to use the open stance can save you approximately 4 to 6 steps in long rallies.

To use the open stance the knees must be flexed in order to maintain proper balance and help in energy release. Take a wide stance with your weight loaded on the back or outside leg so that you can transfer the stored energy from that back leg to the front leg and through the swing. The key ingredient to remember in the open stance is the rotation or coiling of the hips, torso and shoulders. Without it you will have no power on the shot.

You need to be comfortable using both stances at anytime. Use the closed stance when recovery is not an issue or if you're moving in on a short ball or if you choose to drive the ball with force. It takes great footwork to get into position to have a strong stance either open or closed. Try going through an hour of practicing groundstrokes using only the closed stance then try another hour with only the open stance. You'll find that each stance has its own unique footwork that you must own.

Hitting the closed stance, two handed backhand

The Two-Handed Swing

To perform the two-handed swing begin the racquet back by first cocking the wrist so that the racquet head is pointing towards the sky and there is a slight wrinkle in the back of the wrists. Next begin to straighten the dominant arm as the hips, torso and shoulders begin to coil. This is what is known as the loading stage of the stroke where power is being stored.

Next, drop the racquet head in the backswing making sure that the back of your dominant hand is turning away from your body as the racquet head drops into the slot between the hip and the back of the knee or just below the level of the oncoming ball. Now fully loaded, immediately begin to release the stored power by uncoiling the shoulders, hips and torso while snapping the wrists through the hitting zone. Timing is everything at this point and you must be able to pull this off no matter what type of ball your opponent hits at you.

In the photo sequence below you can see all the various stages as well as the release of power as the weight shifts from the back leg up through the point of contact. As the weight shifts the hips and shoulders uncoil and release the stored power gained from the coiling of the shoulders and hips in the backswing. Just like the set up on the forehand the knee of the right leg bends down and into the back left leg. (see photo # 1)

 # 1
early preparation of two-handed backhand

loaded stage of the two-handed backhand

contact point of the two-handed closed stance backhand

finishing stage of the two-handed backhand

This puts the player below the level of the ball and allows him to hit up, drive through or jump into the point of contact. As the body totally uncoils notice how the player's weight has shifted fully to the front leg and his arms have wrapped around his shoulders. This shows the incredible force at which the ball was struck. It is important to note that every ball, no matter what speed you wish to hit, should be struck with accelerated snapping wrists and to vary the ball speed you should strike the ball at different angles. Never ever decelerate through the point of contact with the ball if you are hitting a topspin or driving two-handed backhand stroke.

The One Handed Slice Backhand

The slice backhand is needed in the New Game for different reasons than the two handed topspin backhand. The slice is used three different ways but rarely is it used to end the point.

First and foremost the slice is a great tactical shot when used to move an opponent to a certain area of the court to set up a particular shot you own and want to hit. For example a low deep slice down the sideline can be used to approach the net or to set up a cross-court response allowing you to then drive a forehand shot down the other sideline. Using the slice to set up your big shots is the most offensive way to play the slice.

For her entire career, Steffi Graf used her slice backhand to set up her big forehand. Consequently we all remember her countless winners from her forehand but very few from her backhand. That's because she used her backhand primarily as a set up shot and not as a weapon. She was also very good at playing her slice defensively or in a neutralizing way which are the other two ways to play the slice.

The second way to play the slice is defensively. Because of the increasing power in the New Game there will be times when you just can't get into position to drive the ball and having the ability to slice a powerful groundstroke back deep into the court can buy you time to reposition yourself for a more offensive shot. A defensive slice should have more airtime to it then a driving set up slice to give you that needed time to recover.

Finally the slice is needed at times to neutralize an opponent who is attacking you or who has moved you off the court looking to set you up

for one of their big shots. By having the ability to slice a ball low over the net to various areas of the frontcourt you can neutralize that attack and turn the point in your favor.

See the various stages of the slice backhand in the photos below.

| early preparation of a backhand slice | unloading into the ball on a backhand slice | releasing the wrist through the contact point |

The Slice Grip

If you want to get the most variety out of your slice I suggest you use one hand in a continental grip. This way you can open or close the racquet face to produce different degrees of backspin in order to make the ball skid, check up or stay low. If you must use two hands you still should let go with the non-dominate hand through the contact point to get better feel and control of the shot. The non-dominate hand and arm should be used to set the racquet each time and then be used to balance the body through the shot by extending backwards as far as the follow through of dominant arm goes forward.

The Slice Stance

Use the closed stance position where your feet are perpendicular to the baseline on most backhand slices. This position will give you better balance when you are coiling the hips, shoulders and torso, and allow for the best weight transfer through the hitting phase of the stroke. As your weight transfers and your shoulders, hips and torso uncoil, drag your back foot toe along the ground to keep you anchored and balanced. This will aid you in the pinpoint control of the stroke. If you're making a move forward you may want to slide the back foot and leg in and behind the front leg again for better balance and control. Your stance should be at shoulder width. The open stance can be used when out of position or short on preparation time if you have a good coil of the shoulders and hips. Without the coil your ball flight will likely be high and soft as it's difficult to hit down and through the ball from the open position. Practice both!

The Slice Swing

As soon as you recognize the ball is coming to your backhand, bend the arm and cock the wrist so that the racquet head is pointing up. I like to have that racquet head up as you begin to turn the shoulders to hide the shot from your opponent as long as possible. Also try keeping the dominant arm close to your body as you begin the shoulder, hip and torso coil. This, loading stage of the stroke, is again where power is being stored.

As the ball approaches, there are a lot of ways to take the racquet back. I suggest you try to take the racquet back in a reverse C-loop pattern, which means taking the racquet back through the low zone below the shoulders and then looping it up in the backswing to a point well above the eventual contact with the ball. Any extra shoulder turn that you can squeeze in before you begin the swing forward is great. Try and coil to the point where you feel your back is almost facing the net. Position your head so that you are looking directly over the dominant arm shoulder.

1st stage of the reverse loop backhand slice

2nd stage going above the ball on a reverse loop

coming down into the contact point of a reverse C-style loop slice

In the photos on the previous page you can see the various stages of the reverse C-loop slice swing. As you begin to swing forward and down through the ball, extend your arm as the shoulders, hips and torso begin to uncoil, making the dominant arm straighten out and the non-dominate arm extend behind the body. As you near the contact zone there is a rotation of the forearm and a release of energy stored in the cocked wrist. This technique helps to generate tremendous racquet head speed all while in a long controlled follow through. Your backswing may vary according to the time you have to hit the ball but this release of energy at contact and into the follow though is a necessity no matter what backswing you use. Don't punch at the ball cutting this forearm and wrists release short or your ball will land short and give your opponent the means to attack you.

Top Five Backhand Drills

1. One Side Wonder- This drill is for shot control. The player must alternate his or her shots from corner to corner while the coach hits or feeds every type of shot into the backhand side.

2. Open Stance Crosscourt Angles- This drill highlights the frontcourt angle. The player must hit sharp angles inside the service line area from an open stance position in the backcourt. Practice hitting both two-handed topspin and one-handed slice backhand shots into the angle.

3. Non-Dominate Arm Forehands- The player must hit forehands with the non-dominate arm only. Set the hand slightly higher on the handle or have the player hold a racquet in each hand and only hit forehand topspin shots. This drill improves the coordination of the non-dominate arm and stimulates the left-brain.

4. Four Shot Style Feeds –The coach feeds Four different styles of ball flights and the player must hit the proper wrist snapping counter shot according to the ball flight and ball speed. Start with above the shoulder shots and go down to the ankles. This drill improves ball striking ability and wrists snaps.

5. Slicing Rows- Draw lines across the court that represent different depths from the baseline to the service line. The player must hit a one-handed slice shot into each row created by the lines. This drill improves feel and depth control of the slice backhand. Coaches should number the rows and then call out a number as you feed in a ball.
(See drill pages for backhand drills, 1 & 2)

❖ *The Venus & Serena Factor* ❖

One of the ways that Venus & Serena learned both backhands so effectively was by dedicating entire practice sessions to only using either the slice backhand or the two-handed topspin backhand.

From the first backhand hit to the last backhand hit they would stick with only one backhand, as we would go through all our normal drills and point playing games. Now knowing how competitive these two girls are you might think that in order to ensure winning a practice point they would hit a driving topspin even if it was an all-slice day or a slice backhand even if it was an all two-handed topspin day. Well they wouldn't. They instead always accepted the challenge of only using just one of their backhands, which in turn made them learn new ways to win points. It was a very important layer in their game strategy.

Coach's Notebook

Early Ages (5-9)—Begin backhand development with a straight back racquet backswing. Focus mostly on the two-handed grip and the contact point with the ball being out in front. It's better to start in a closed stance until stronger to make sure balance and early preparation of the shoulder, hip and torso coil are established. This is usually the stronger side for a while so take advantage of that fact and begin introducing different spins and adding power. Add lots of power. I think that all young players should always try, and be taught, to hit the ball hard. If you learn a slow controlled swing at a young age it will be hard to unlearn it when you want to swing harder. Two-handed slice backhands are fine at this time but as strength is developed you should try and drop the non-dominant arm. Practice the fundamentals of all your stroke rigorously!

Jr Tournament Level Player—Get going on the open stance backhands needed to handle any wide or deeply hit ball. Make sure to develop accelerated wrist snaps through the point of contact and practice the same four wrist snaps you learned on the forehand. Start establishing a one-handed slice backhand on all low balls that are not drivable or for defensive and neutralizing situations. Begin to establish different ball flights to all areas of the court by using different degrees of spin. Learn to take away and add pace to any ball. Practice adding power to balls with no pace and neutralizing balls with pace. If not one of your weapons then the backhand needs to be your more consistent side or set up side.

Pro Player Beginnings—Now that you've established your backhand as a weapon look for new ways to win points off this stroke. If you're already powerful start using more angles, spins, drops and feel shots in practice to add variety. If you're already showing a lot of variety try to add more power. Don't sit back and think you are done developing this stroke either. You should be able to use your slice backhand all three ways: to set yourself up, to play defense and to neutralize. Go entire practice sessions only using your backhand slice or only using your two-handed backhand. You should own at least five different ways to win points off your backhand side.

CHAPTER FIVE

The Return of Serve

The return of serve has become almost as much a weapon as the serve in the New Game. Players are more then ever taking command of a point by ripping a return into a corner off of a weak or poorly placed serve. Gone is the thought of playing defensively on returns and alive is the attitude of being an offensive returnee. To do this you must maintain an aggressive attitude. It is easy for a coach to say to a player, "Be aggressive on the returns today," but unless that player owns his or her return game those words are useless. How do you own your return game? Practice, practice, practice. Spend as much time as is needed so that you can return a variety of serving styles to every part of the court. Then when you get good at returning all those serving styles, find five more players whose serving styles differ and master those and so on and so on.

When it comes to the return game, it's those players who are able to handle and place all three serves (slice, flat, kick), delivered at various speeds and angles, by both right handed and left handed players, on all different surfaces that every server trying to hold serve fears. To be that player follow this return game recipe.

Ready Position

Establish yourself as a threat by taking a low ready position. Starting low sends an immediate message to the server that you are ready for anything they fire at you. It is also a **key fundamental** ingredient for success as mentioned in chapter one. You'll be able to see the ball better as it comes across the net and be able to handle any type of bounce.

You are allowed to set up anywhere you like but try lining yourself up so that your shoulders are squared to the server with your feet right at the baseline/singles sideline corner area. As the match progresses you may want to change this positioning according to your opponents serving patterns and speed. Try repositioning yourself in different areas for different point and game situations to apply more pressure on your opponent or to protect a particular side of yours that is being picked on. A player with a weak first serve for example should have you inside the baseline looking to take the ball early and aggressively. A player with a strong serve may have you a step or two behind the baseline.

Also, if your forehand has developed into a big time shot, start in a forehand grip with your non-dominate hand ready to adjust the racquet for all backhand returns. Try moving your ready position a step to the backhand side to make the forehand side appear more open. This way you bait your opponent to serve more serves to your forehand side giving you more shots to your weapon side. If your backhand side is your weapon then try moving your ready position a step to the forehand side to get more backhand returns.

return ready position

Split Step on the Toss

Once you have yourself positioned properly you then need to get your weight moving forward by stepping forward and split stepping onto your toes just as the server tosses the ball into the air. Time your split step so that you land just as the server strikes the ball. If you anticipate a weak serve or just want to take the ball even earlier then your normal return, try taking two or more forward steps before the split step. Be careful not to get caught moving without any time for a split step though or you'll be unable to lunge to the sides to cover wide serves to each wing.

You can't afford to be flat footed on the return of serve. The pros know this and have precise footwork routines or rituals they go through before each and every serve is hit. Whether it's a right foot, left foot, right foot pattern or a slight shuffling of the feet side to side or stepping a dance pattern or simply shifting weight from one foot to the other all done just before the server tosses the ball; they know they would rather be on their toes and moving forward then to get caught standing still or backing up. Yes every player has their own footwork ritual they go through to get themselves ready for the return of serve—What's yours?

Shorten the Backswing

Big serves mean one thing, less time to react. Unless you have the hand eye speed of Lleyton Hewitt or Justine Henin-Hardenne, I suggest you shorten your backswing and focus more on making solid contact with the ball out in front of your body with just a quick wrist and forearm snap or an abbreviated loop motion. You can practice getting quicker at reacting by having your coach or practice partner serve at you from the service line instead of the baseline, but even as you do get better at returning you still should shorten your backswing to take time away from your opponent who remember still has to recover after delivering their serve. If you're still struggling to make solid contact with the ball try starting further back behind the baseline. Make sure to leave room for your footwork ritual so that you can still have a sense of moving into even the biggest of serves.

Placement or Depth

Placement is great but depth rules! Sure you want to be able to place returns all over your opponent's side of the net but if your return consistently hits near or on the baseline you have taken away any advantage gained from the server who has hit a big serve but elected to stay back. Even if you have to block the ball back, try to get depth by giving your ball flight some extra airtime so you will have extra time to recover to the middle of the court.

When returning to a serve and volley style player you'll need a shorter return that gets down at the servers charging feet. I'll tell you this though, the days of the true serve and volley players are gone. Why? Because of how much more aggressive the return game has become. Servers today just can't take the risk of coming in on any average serve. Players in the New Game are returning winners more consistently on all types of servers and on all types of serves, something that just didn't happen in the past. Racquet technology has helped attributed to this fact, cutting down on the shanks and mis-hits that use to happen regularly with the old frames, as had strength and fitness training, which has created stronger more athletic players. Replacing the true serve and volley player though, is the all-court player who will stay back and rally but looks to aggressively come to the net when the opportunity invites. I don't think you will ever see another serve and volley singles player on the women's tour—yes you can quote me.

Get Aggressive

Once you've gauged your opponent's serve it's time to get aggressive with it. After your footwork ritual and a split step you should find yourself with your weight shifted forward onto your toes and the oncoming serve quickly approaching—now lunge and rip! Being an aggressive returnee is as much a mental attitude as it is a practiced skill. You need to practice attacking and swinging all out on all three types of serves, (flat,

slice, kick) as all have slight bounce differences that you will need to adjust to as you are moving in on them. Being able to take your game to your opponent right from the return is mandatory in the New Game. Once you start connecting solidly on a few of your opponents fastest serves then you'll find you'll have the confidence to move inside the baseline even further the next time.

To lunge effectively on a return of serve, you'll need to do what I call, the kick step. The kick step is when your lunge foot kicks up high behind you after you have lunged into and as you are striking the return. If you're right handed and hitting a forehand return it will be your right foot that you will lunge off of and kick up behind you and if you are hitting a backhand it will be your left foot. Practice this first by having your coach or practice partner serve you slow serves. As you get better at lunging and kicking on those slower serves then speed it up to first serves.

You may think you have a great return game right now, and maybe you do. But know this; there are over a hundred thousand players out there right now who you've never played against, all practicing to join the world of professional tennis and all who will serve slightly different to you. For this reason you need to practice returning serves everyday so that you will always own your return game no matter what type of serve is hit at you. Like your forehand, your return game needs to be a weapon. That makes two weapons you'll need in the New Game — so far.

Top Five Return Drills

1. Serves from the service line/Colored ball drill-Just like it sounds; your coach or practice partner serves at you from the service line instead of the baseline. The use of colored balls adds focus to the drill. The player must holler the color of the ball served before hitting it. This drill helps quicken your hand eye speed coordination.

2. Returns right back at you—One of the best returns for accuracy is the return right back at the server. It's easier to return a serve back in the same direction it was delivered rather then change the direction. If the depth is good the server must have good footwork in order to get out of the way. This should be a lunge, kick and rip it drill!

3.When Wide go Wider—Have your coach or practice partner serve flat and slice balls out wide so that you can practice returning the wide ball with an even wider angle onto your opponents side of the net. This is Serena's favorite return from the deuce court.

4. Chip or Rip—When returning weak serves you must be aggressive. To do this move inside the baseline, closer then normal, and practice ripping balls on the rise to all areas of the court. Then to add variety to your aggressive game practice chipping deep and rushing the net on those same types of serves as well as chipping short drop shot returns.

5. Lunge-Kick Step —This drill will make your return game an aggressive weapon. This technique, I guarantee, will maximize the amount of power you can put into your return. Have your coach or practice partner serve to you. Start in a low ready position just behind the baseline, then take one or two steps forward to get your upper body weight moving forward, then split step onto your toes, then lunge forward and kick up your lunge foot of whichever side you are hitting from behind you while snapping your racquet head with maximum speed into the oncoming ball. You have just performed the lunge-kick step.

Question: Which collision is more violent; two trains that are going at maximum velocity that ram into each other or one train at maximum velocity ramming into a wall? Answer: the two trains because there is speed coming from both sources. Think about that as you are moving forward to rip the next oncoming serve.

(SEE DRILL PAGES for explanation of return drill #1)

❖ *The Venus & Serena Factor* ❖

One area where Venus & Serena constantly put the most fear into their opponents is on the return of serve. Just watch one of their next matches and look where they stand to take the first serve and then watch how they move up almost to the service box to receive the second serve. It's very intimidating!

To be able to do that they practiced returns a few different ways to develop the hand-eye skills and racquet speed skills needed. One drill was the serve from the service line drill mentioned above and another was playing points from inside the baseline and not being allowed to move back. Both these drills made Venus & Serena have quicker reflexes, better forward movement and a great ability to pick up the ball faster off the opponents racquet. But the drill that I believe set them apart was on returning second serves.

Next time you watch either of the sisters play watch where they stand to return second serves. They not only move forward but they also move inward towards the center of the court. A return ready position that they practiced regularly to dare servers to go for that outside sideline area. It took a lot of practice to get use to that court position because it brought a lot of serves into their bodies but the advantages of not having to recover much because of being more in the middle of the court after the return and the missed attempts by servers trying to hit that small open sideline area allowed them to be even more aggressive.

Girls playing Venus & Serena know they better make a lot of first serves or else they'll spend the entire day watching their second serves get crushed.

Coach's Notebook:

Early Ages (5-9)—Begin return development with the fundamentals of the low ready position and with a return target that is high over the middle of the net. A coaches' first drill should be to serve softly from the service line using different colored balls to train the player's eyes to focus on the ball. Players should begin with a simple, short, straight back backswing on both return sides. Make sure that balance and early preparation are established before practicing lunge returns. Make consistency a habit but always practice hitting with power. Remember power is learned easier when young. Practice the five fundamentals!

Jr Tournament Level Player—Practice forward lunging into most returns. Become skilled at hitting returns to all areas of the court off both sides. Know how to block returns as well as slice and chip. Begin to establish an aggressive position on or inside the baseline and learn to lunge, kick step and rip all weak serves. Practice angle returns and down the line returns off both sides and make the return right back at the server a standard. Focus on reading the server and learn to recognize serving patterns during matches.

Pro Player Beginnings—Make sure you are taking control of the point off the return of any weak serve. Develop the ability to hit winners off weak second serves. Be skilled enough to consistently return 90% of all serves using either topspin, under spin or a blocked swing. Have at least five ways to set up the point off the return. Practice trying to move in closer to the net to return serves more on the rise. You must make your return a weapon.

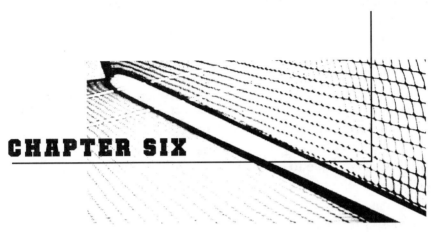

CHAPTER SIX

The Volley

The volley is probably the easiest shot to learn. So why then are there so many bad volleyers? I've watched many aggressive style baseliners over the years who refuse to come to the net or who look foolish when they're at the net because they never took the time to own their volley. And it's not that any of these players found the volley a difficult stroke to hit but rather they found using the volley tactically within their game plan to be the difficult task. Junior players often have a fear of having to leave the security of their baseline game and end the point or have the fear of a passing shot, which is often deemed embarrassing. If you start approaching the net at an early enough age then you'll get use to seeing shots pass by you and it won't bother you as much as it does the seasoned player who is just starting to add a net game to their overall game plan.

All players know this; if you learn to hit big serves or big groundstrokes from the baseline then face it, you are going to get a lot of short balls from your opponents, inviting you to come to the net. Having a solid volley to end the point, and that's almost always what a volley is, a point

ending shot, is well worth the extra practice time. Let's go over some key ingredients to help make every one of your volleys count.

The Grip

The grip I recommend for all volleys is the continental grip. The same grip that I like all players to use for the serve. This grip is found by placing the racquet on its edge and then placing the 'V' of your hand made by the thumb and the index finger on the top of the handle. It's the perfect grip because you don't have to change it when going from a forehand volley to a backhand volley. Junior players, if you're still volleying with two hands on your backhand side try to start dropping the non-dominate hand off in practice. You're only using two hands because of a strength problem so the best way to get stronger is by using only one hand in practice. There is more feel and variety with one hand anyway. Go ahead and use two hands on your backhand swing volley though, as the extra wrist snap power is needed. To get depth and pop on a regular one-handed volley, squeeze the grip on the handle firmly just before contact. To take power off a ball try loosening your grip pressure right before contact with the ball.

The Stance

With your shoulders squared to the net take a low wide stance that has a split step built into it so that after every volley you hit there is an immediate split step to ready yourself for the next shot. Try to make a crossover step every time you go to hit the ball but if there's no time then make sure you turn your shoulders and hips. **Footwork and staying down are key Fundamental ingredients** for success at the net.

When making contact try and have the handle of your racquet directly above your front foot. There will be plenty of times however when you don't have time to crossover and must volley using just a short turn and quick hands. To be ready for those hot shots get low and wait with the racquet head pointing up and slightly to the backhand side. Know this; you'll probably hit at least twenty-five percent more backhand volleys over your tennis playing career because of all the shots at your body that you'll only be able to fend off if you take them as backhand volleys.

To practice getting into a good low stance at the net have your coach or practice partner roll balls to each side of you. To pick the balls up you must split step then do a crossover step while picking up the ball then split step again. Repeat this drill on both sides and soon you'll be able to get low enough to handle any volley and you'll have the footwork to go along with it.

The Backswings

Time is the key element when volleying and usually there is none. For that reason there should be no backswing either. Slightly turn your shoulders and then hips so that your weight shifts to the outside foot of the side of the oncoming ball. Don't take the racquet back past your ears! By turning the shoulders and hips the racquet will already be on the side of your body. Now just lean the face of the racquet into the path of the ball and apply some backspin by driving the bottom edge of the racquet down and through the back of the ball.

On the forehand side keep your non-dominate hand up but out of the hitting zone. This will help you stay balanced but also act as a reference point for hitting the ball out in front of you.

forehand volley contact

The move to the backhand side is also short. The racqet is drawn back by the non-dominate hand, which helps to position the racqet head in preparation for the forward move to contact with the ball. As you make the move to contact on the backhand side try spreading your arms to the exact same lengths in the opposite directions. This will help again with balance and in hitting the ball in front of your body.

the contact point and stance of a
backhand volley

backhand volley

The Forward Swing

The forward swing should be very compact. A short punch while positioning the racquet face for direction is all that is needed. Make contact out in front of your body. Lead through the contact of the ball with the bottom edge of the racquet head. This will help you in your placement of the shot and also apply some backspin to your ball so that it stays low and forces your opponent to hit the next shot up to you.

forehand volley contact

The Swing Volley

What a fun shot this is to hit! Why? Because it is basically your biggest groundstroke you can hit without letting the ball bounce. It's like two jet airplanes colliding in the air—your full swing and your opponent's ball that hasn't lost any steam from bouncing on the ground.

There is some major risk as timing becomes critical. You have to mentally attack this ball like you would any of your big topspin groundstrokes by taking the same big backswing and having the same big follow through. The key ingredient is racquet speed, lots of racquet speed. Without racquet speed your shot may fly over the backcourt fence. The wrist snap used to produce the racquet speed all depends on the height of the ball at contact. You should practice this shot until you can execute it off any height of ball. Remember this is the most aggressive volley you can hit so once you have committed to hitting it in a point don't chicken out half way through the swing.

the take off of a swing volley

the follow through of the
swing volley

❖ *The Venus & Serena Factor* ❖

A lot of girls on tour use the swing volley for balls above their head, some like Kim Clistjers use it more then overheads, but none use it as often or as aggressively as Venus and Serena.

They have always loved to hit the ball hard and the swing volley is one shot you just can't hit lightly or try to finesse so it became a shot that both girls began always looking to move forward and hit.

Serena likes to take her swing volley inside out or straight ahead while Venus likes to go mostly crosscourt with her swing volleys. In their doubles matches together, both will attempt swing volleys on just about any ball hit near them high at the net.

The girls on tour have learned that floating a ball back to the middle of the court is just not an option against Venus or Serena, as they will quickly and aggressively move forward to hit the swing volley for a winner. Because that option is taken away it forces players to try high-risk shots that most often lead to errors.

In the early years, practicing the swing volley had a two-fold effect on Venus & Serena. It helped develop good wrists snaps and it taught them to hit the ball out in front of them for added control. Both necessary ingredients for their powerful baseline groundstrokes.

When to go to the Net?

That is a question that almost every player I've ever coached has asked me at one time or another and my answer is always the same, "Every chance you get!" Why? Because in the New Game of all-court aggressive baseline basher tennis where every ball is hit with maximum power, spin and depth, your opportunities to rush the net are far less then they use to be. Let's take a look at my top five times to rush the net.

Top Five Times to Rush the Net

1. When you get a short ball. Your opponent has hit a ball that lands around the service line pulling you inside the baseline. These short balls now become approach shots as they offer an excellent opportunity to get you to the net and under your terms. Most of the time you should take that approach shot down the line with control or keep it in front of you to set yourself up for the volley winner but if you're playing on a fast surface going crosscourt to the open court can be just as beneficial.

2. Over Powering an Opponent with a Deep Groundstroke. If you've hit a penetrating groundstroke that lands anywhere near the baseline, preferably in a corner, you should step inside the baseline and look for a swing volley opportunity off your opponents probable weak shot. If your opponent is consistently hitting short then you must be overpowering them with your strokes and shots and should be ready to approach the net often.

3. When you're serving at 40-0. The score always matters in how aggressive you can be in a match and when you're serving at 40-0 you have the green light to be overly aggressive. A serve and volley executed perfectly can really crush an opponent mentally and give you the edge the rest of the match especially if you don't normally serve and volley.

4. Your Opponent can't pass you. Let's say you've already come to the net a few times during the set on approach shots and each time your opponent couldn't execute a pass or a lob even though they seem to have good strokes and shots when you're rallying from the baseline. It may be the pressure of you at the net that is producing the errors from your opponent and if that's the case then you should go to the net more often and keep applying the pressure.

5. When Returning at 0-40. No server likes to be broken at love and what's worse is when a known baseliner wins that break point at the net. So take a chance at 0-40 and chip and charge or rip it and charge the net. If you execute a perfect volley your opponent will be dejected and your confidence will go up and if you don't execute you are still up two points and can try again or play your normal aggressive baseline game. You might be able to bluff your opponent into making an error just by charging the net.

Top Five Volley Drills

1. **Two on One Volleys**—Two baseline players hit a variety of spins and speeds at a player positioned at the net. Play games of fifteen points before switching.

2. **Volley Catch**-Two players volleying soft to medium controlled volleys from the service line. On the 5th ball one player must catch the shot with his or her racquet strings. It takes awfully soft hands.

3. **Make a 'V'**- There are two V's to make when practicing your volleys. One V is in the positioning of your racquet arm before contact with the ball and the second V is in the pattern the feet move in when you step across and into the forehand volley and then recover and step across and in to hit a backhand volley.

4. **Degrees of Backspin**-Stand at the net and practice hitting drop volleys with a slightly more open racquet face on every five balls or so until you can hit a drop volley that returns to your side of the net after bouncing on your opponent's side. This is a fun shot to hit and it develops great racquet feel.

5.7 **Zone Volleys**-There are seven zones you need to be able to hit both forehand and backhand volleys into. Frontcourt, midcourt and backcourt. (See Drill Pages for volley drill #5)

Coach's Notebook:

Early Ages (5-9)—Coaches should begin by tossing balls from your hand or hitting soft balls to the forehand volley establishing the importance of holding the racquet head up while at the net. It's important not to scare your player away from the net at an early age by hitting at them too hard. Don't hit volleys for very long as holding the racquet head up gets tiring and is not as much fun for young players. Let them swing away at this point but encourage the punch stroke. Stress the importance of the footwork and of making contact out in front. Practice volleying balloons back and forth for a fun drill for all players.

Jr Tournament Level Player—You should be skilled at hitting your forehand and backhand volleys to various zones of the court from various positions at the net. Begin adding a little under spin to most of your volleys for some added zip and skip. Practice ending points by hitting angle and drop volleys during point situations. Practice attacking mid-court floaters with a swing volley and approaching the net on all short balls. If you want to consider yourself an aggressive baseliner then you must be approaching the net on all short balls and have the volley ability to end the point. You can't force the action if you don't have a volley game.

Pro Player Beginnings—To be a good volleyer you need to have good hands. Your volley practice should consist of quick reaction drills against a variety of spins and speeds. If you can't find the time to practice your volley game just play more doubles. If you have developed a volley game then you need to use it in your singles matches but be selective in your approaches to the net as all players in the New Game can hit passing shots. A short ball of any sort is always an invitation to approach the net and at this stage of your game that approach shot placement is more of a concern then your volley. If your approaches are penetrating then you'll look like the greatest volleyer that ever was because your opponent's responses will be weak and predictable but if your approaches are short and weak then no matter how good your volley game is you will get passed.

CHAPTER SEVEN

The Serve

OK, so how good do you really want to be? Did you practice your serve today? If you answered you want to play pro-level tennis but no you didn't work on your serve today then I suggest you stop reading this book right now because it won't do you any good. Because if you didn't practice your serve today I can guarantee you won't go far as a professional tennis player.

The serve is the one single stroke that can take you higher on the world tennis ladder more than any other, and that is no exaggeration. Know this: when you are serving you are in control of the tennis match and everything that goes on in and around that match. Just imagine for a moment that you're playing at the French Open and you step up to the baseline to serve the first game of the match. Everyone watching in the stands and on TV, your opponent, all the linesmen, all the ball kids, the chair umpire, all the camera crews and all the press stop to watch you deliver your first serve. You must admit that's a pretty awesome scene that you just imagined and it happens over and over again every time you step up to serve.

Power or Placement

A serve with power is a great thing to have but know this: your power level has its limits, and once you've reached that limit you must have something else that keeps your opponent from attacking your serve. That something else is spin, variety and placement.

I've seen a lot of players with average power in their serves who still had successful tennis careers all because they could pinpoint their placement and because they had the ability to hit three different serves at anytime. Don't get me wrong; I believe power should be a constant career goal in your serving practice. There's no better way to get yourself out of a serving jam then to have the ability to overpower an opponent, but if you only have one type of serve it doesn't matter how hard you hit it because your opponent will eventually groove in on it and be ready anyway. The bottom line is three serves are better then one.

My advice is to start out by learning the flat serve first since this is the serve that will eventually become your most powerful serve, and then the slice serve and finally the kick serve. Once you have developed all three serves your next task is to develop the ability to place each serve into all areas of the service boxes. Once that skill has been achieved you should continue to look for areas to pump up your serve to make it an unreturnable shot. The serve is the third and finally weapon that is mandatory in the New Game. So I ask you again, did you practice some aspect of your serve today?

The Flat Serve

The flat serve technique is performed by hitting the back of the ball with a pronating wrist so that the string bed of the racquet face is flat on the ball at the contact point producing a serve with maximum power and no spin. The ball toss for the flat serve should be straight out in front of the lead foot at least one racquet length in front of the baseline. The ball toss placement is very important for serving consistency. For this reason I recommend that you practice your toss as much as you do your serve motion.

For flat serve toss practice lay another racquet on the court extending out from the toe of your lead foot. Then toss the ball two inches higher then you can reach with your racquet over your head and out in front so that the ball will land on the sweet spot of the racquet lying on the court. Next practice the toss using your entire service motion, doing everything you would normally do in your service motion except hitting the ball. Again try to hit the center of the racquet on the court.

The flat serve should be a weapon, your big gun, your fastball. When you want to announce your presence with authority this is the serve you want to do it with. When the flat serve is on you are like a baseball pitcher whose throwing nothing but fastball strikes. The problems can be that the flat serve can go off the strike zone and become a low percentage serve or it can be that some players get grooved on and like returning nothing but fastballs. And that's why you need to have three serves so you can then be that fastball pitcher who also has a curveball and a knuckler.

The Service Motion

The service motion that I recommend is the step-up motion. Why? Because the step-up motion not only provides a means of getting a good weight transfer into the contact point but it also provides good rhythm from the loading phase through to the follow through. To perform the step-up motion, follow this five-step recipe:

Start with your feet shoulder width apart and at a 45 degree angle to the baseline. On the backswing pick up your back foot and move it back slightly to brace your stance for the weight shift that takes place as your shoulders, torso and hips begin to coil into the energy loading phase of the serve. This step should be as short or as long as what feels most comfortable. What's important is that your step back is rhythmic with your swing. Once the coil and weight shift back has begun, pick up the back foot and bring it up and along side the lead foot as you coil your body completely and go into a deep knee bend. As your weight is now shifting forward, toss the ball and prepare to release all the stored energy up and into the ball. As your wrist snap accelerates the racquet to the ball, uncoil your torso, hips and shoulders while jumping up to the ball toss and into the court. Land inside the baseline on your lead foot, left foot for righties, and follow through so that you look as if you are bowing to the opponent.

early preparation of the
step-up serve

the loaded stage of the
step-up serve

unloading into contact
on the step-up serve

The Slice Serve

When the surface is faster the slice serve takes over as the first serve of choice. Why? Because the slice spin becomes exaggerated by the faster surface making the ball skid lower and faster. Just watch Wimbledon this year and you'll see a lot of players substitute their normal flat first serves with slice because of the slick fast grass surface.

To hit the slice serve effectively imagine the back of the ball as the face of a clock. Make contact on the ball at the three o'clock part of the ball if you are a right-hander and the nine o'clock piece of the ball if you are a lefty. Use a continental grip so that you can get plenty of angle on the strings of the racquet and snap the wrist forward with a loose flick leading into the ball with the edge of the racquet head.

As you get better at hitting the slice serve try varying your contact on the ball from two o'clock to five o'clock. You'll get different degrees of spin and be able to hit to slightly different service box areas. Also without making it obvious to the returnee try tossing your ball toss a little further to the right for righties and further to the left for lefties. This will magnify the amount of spin your slice serve will have although if recognized it will also send a signal to the receiver of what type of serve is coming. It's best to be able to hit all your first serves from the same toss.

If you are a lefty you must own the slice serve for the simple reason that the spin of the ball goes away from a righty's backhand side, which is generally the weaker side. Lefties also have the advantage of using their slice serve to swing an opponent wide in the Ad-court, which is where most games come to an end.

Whether you're a righty or a lefty, one of the best times to use the slice serve is after a very long baseline rally. Why? Because your opponent may still be winded or tired from the long point just played making it hard for them to pick up their feet to go get your wide swinging serve. You can sometimes pick up a quick point from a lazy returnee if you remember to hit the slice out wide after long points.

| lining up for the Wimbledon slice serve | contacting over the center of the court on the slice Wimbledon serve | the finish of the slice serve |

On the side where you can't swing your opponent wide, deuce court for lefties and ad-court for righties, try this slicing serve technique that I call the Wimbledon Serve. First inch up as close as you can to the service hash mark on the baseline. Then toss your serve toss across the mark and into the other half of the court. Without foot-faulting, lunge over and hit your slice serve so that when you land you are well into the court on the opposite side. Watch how your slice serve will spin down the centerline and then quickly away from your opponent for an ace.

The Kick Serve

The kick serve or topspin serve is the standard second serve for most high level players. It's very effective on soft clay courts because of the fact that the spin of the ball dives sharply and bounces irregularly high. That diving topspin makes for a high percentage serve with still the chance of getting some free points if your opponent doesn't time the high bounce

properly. To effectively return the kick serve a player must take the ball as it is rising so that it doesn't get above shoulder height. Balls that bounce higher then the shoulders are tougher to control and are also much tougher to add power to.

To hit the kick serve try this technique. Move your grip slightly to a one-handed backhand topspin grip. Toss your serve toss back over your head but slightly in front of your backhand side. Arch your back and tilt your head as you coil up so that you can see the six o'clock to nine o'clock part of the ball to hit. Hit up through the bottom of the ball trying to snap your strings up and over the top of the ball while pulling across the back of the ball at the same time. Completely finish the swing so that the palm of your racquet hand is facing up so that you could balance a ball on the strings of your racquet. Experiment by hitting slightly different bottom and side areas of the ball to produce different heights over the net and different degrees of kick spin on the ball.

loading up for a kick serve   **reaching up into contact on a kick serve**   **the finish of a kick serve**

Top Five Serving Drills

1. **Serve from the service line**—This drill improves a player's wrist snap and racquet speed. Each day make 30 serves at full speed from the service line.

2.**8 cone Zones**—Place 4 cones in each box (2 for the wide sides, 1 for into the body and 1 for down the middle on the 'T'. Practice hitting each cone with each of your three serves.

3. **Serving Horse**—-Divide the service box into 3 zones. Call your placement and serve type before you serve. If you miss you get a letter and if you make it then your coach or practice partner must make it or he or she gets a letter.

4. **Copycat**—-Divide the service box into 5 zones. Your coach or practice partner goes first and hits a certain serve type into a zone. You have to copy exactly.

5.**Lines only**—-Practice aiming for the lines by hitting one type of serve (flat, slice, kick) onto all five lines of the two service boxes. Once you do one serve type switch to another type and so on. If you are on clay court sweep the clay over the lines to see the marks better.

(See drill pages for serving drill #2)

❖ The Venus & Serena Factor ❖

To date; Venus Williams still owns the record for the fastest serve on the WTA. Serena, who is behind in power, owns one of the most lethally placed serves, the slice serve out wide to the deuce side.

Again Venus's early development of power allowed her to hit big serves to win points and to hit that record breaking serve while Serena's lack of power forced her to learn how to place her serves more effectively to win points.

Ask the players on the WTA whose serve is better and you'll get a mixed bag of answers. It all depends on the style of player you ask. All agree though if you were to combine Venus's power with Serena's placement you would have an unstoppable weapon.

One reason both Venus and Serena have great serves is because of the early development of wrist snap they learned by taking their old tennis racquets and throwing them as high and as far as they could through the air using their service motions. Some practice days the girls would spend thirty minutes each out in the empty field next to their home courts throwing old tennis rackets. They learned right away that if you want distance, which is power, then you must snap your wrist.

To this day when I see Venus or Serena serve I can imagine them throwing their old racquets. I hope they don't forget during a match and accidentally let go.

Coach's Notebook:

Early Ages (5-9)—Begin with the ball toss. Practice a high toss that goes above your head as high as you can reach with your racquet plus two inches and lands inside the baseline one racquet length in front of your left foot. The toss is a major part of the serve but it doesn't get enough attention at this age. Most kids don't have the patience to stand and practice tossing over and over again. But if learned, it will save a player three times as much practice later on. Next begin hitting flat serves from the service line area until you have a strong enough wrist snap to move back to the baseline. Don't be worried about results and instead focus on the swing motion technique. The grip is the last piece to the puzzle and should be in an eastern forehand grip until strong enough to move to continental grip. Wrist Snap and racquet speed should always be a focal point. Don't even try to hit kick serves until there is proper shoulder and wrists strength. The demands of the kick serve are too great for underdeveloped muscles and you don't want to run the risk of injury to the shoulder area. In baseball youth leagues it is common knowledge not to teach the curveball, for the same reasons that the motion of that pitch puts great demands on the shoulder and arm, to a young pitcher until proper shoulder strength is developed.

Jr Tournament Level Player—If you haven't made the grip change into a continental grip then do so now. You need to have the technique down of all three serves: flat, slice and kick. You may not own all three yet but you should be practicing each one daily and trying all three in your tournament matches. Power should be slightly more of a concern then placement at this stage of your development. Work on tossing your ball more into the court so that you can increase the wrist snap speed as well as get more power from your legs. Be willing to lose some service games because you are trying to hit more powerful serves. I was once asked, "What does a powerful serve look like?" The answer is that all your serves should look like an act of violence between your racquet and the ball that takes place like a flash of lightning.

Pro Player Beginnings—The power in your serve should be either fully developed or almost fully developed and now placement takes the front seat. You now need to practice hitting serves that disrupt your opponents return games and to do that you must be able to hit any serve to any spot in the service boxes. Practice setting up shot combinations that start with your serves. Can you win your service games? If not then there are only two things it could be at this stage of your game. You either need more power or better placement. Don't ever settle and say that your serve is as good as it can be, because your serve can always be improved upon and as a pro it is a must if you ever want to win Wimbledon.

CHAPTER EIGHT

Futuremetrics

For many players, this may be the most important chapter of this book. I believe that everyone has within their self a certain amount of natural talent for their chosen sport, some much more then others, and others much less than some. And that talent, once maximized, cannot and will not go any higher then what that person has within them. They will eventually reach their ceiling of natural talent, in other words.

As a tennis player you too will, at some point in your career, reach your natural talent ceiling of your ball striking and shot making skills. But does that mean once your ceiling is reached that you will never be able to improve your game? Not at all. Improving ones athletic ability is the answer to raising that ceiling. And since you can always improve in this area, then the sky is the limit as to how much better of a player you can become.

In the 1990's I was coaching a few players that collectively all needed to improve their athletic ability. They were all good ball strikers with good tactical minds but lacked the athleticism needed to take them deep into the draws of big tournaments and on to the highest levels of this game. I believed this was from their lack of playing alternate sports as children and in their non-specific off court training programs.

By playing or practicing the skills of alternate sports, I believe, you can add a multitude of benefits to your fine motor skills, which will then add to your tennis game skills. For example: going to a batting cage and hitting baseballs off both sides of your body (right and left side) will enhance your hand eye ball striking and swing skills or going to the gym and playing some one-on-one basketball will help you in your agility, movement and body strength or playing soccer will aid in your speed and footwork quickness or going to the driving range and trying to put topspin and slice on a few dozen golf shots will help your swing weight shift and fine motor movements of the hands and arms. Watch as all your athletic skills become enhanced not to mention the fact that it will add the ingredient of **fun** into your off court training program.

What my players needed then was an off court training program that incorporated those skills of the various other sports to help them improve their tennis athletic skills which in turn would improve their on-court performance and eventually their match results. Since I have always been a subscriber to the theory that if you work hard at improving your athletic ability you will in turn improve what ever sport you are involved in, I took up the task to put together a program. I took drills from my college basketball days, summer baseball leagues, backyard football games, track and field practices and every other sport that I had competed in or practiced over the years, added in the latest plyometric drills and resistance strength training techniques and what I came up with was an off-court aerobic training program which I call Futuremetrics.

What is Futuremetrics?

Futuremetrics is an off-court aerobic training program that is designed to improve a player's speed, strength, agility, power and endurance, using the athletic skills needed in various other sports to help cross train for tennis specific athletic skills, all performed in a fun and positive atmosphere.

For you coaches, the last part of that sentence, a fun and positive atmosphere, is the key to any off-court training program. Most players want to improve their athleticism but if it means running in circles for an hour around a track or on a treadmill or doing a uninteresting weight room workout most just don't have the time nor the discipline to make it happen.

But if the training program is as enjoyable to them as being on the tennis court is, well, then a player will likely work much harder at improving his or her athleticism and reap the athletic benefits which will then show in his or her on court performance.

For you players, think about this: when your tennis career is all over, if you worked hard in your off-court training to develop those additional fine motor athletic skills, then you'll get to take those skills with you into whatever sport or career you choose to enjoy next. You'll also learn a lot about how to keep your body healthy and in the best possible shape. I bet then, you'll be glad that you developed those additional athletic skills and went through the pain of an off-court aerobic training program, instead of just being a good on-court ball striker.

Additional advantages of a good off-court aerobic training program:

More general physical endurance
A stronger heart
More red blood cells carrying oxygen to the tissue, which means a slower heart rate with more rest between beats. (A heart beating 80 beats per minute beats 115000 times a day; a heart beating 50 beats per minute only beats 72,000 times a day. A savings of 43,000 beats.)
More muscle strength
Better resistance to disease
Decrease in body fat
Lower blood pressure
Increase of endorphins, which are natural brain stimulators
Reduced stress and depression
Increased self-esteem

The following is a sample four-week Futuremetrics program that I use with my players in South Florida. It begins and ends with a 10-15 minute stretching routine.

A Four-Week Futuremetrics Schedule

The Stretch Routine

It only takes about 10-15 minutes to stretch your primary muscles and increase flexibility, which can often be the most important factor in keeping you injury free. Flexibility helps your speed, quickness and power during exercise and so increasing it should be a constant goal in your training. The pre-exercise stretch, I believe, should not be performed as deep as the during-exercise stretch or the post-exercise stretch. It is important to warm the muscles up before aerobic exercise but not to over-stretch the muscles. With some players, stretching can help achieve a proper warm-up but in others it may actually increase their risk of injury and reduce their potential strength during physical exercise. There are many new studies in this area and all state that each player is different in the area of the pre-exercise stretch. You may want to experiment with deep and light stretching as well as not stretching at all before each session. All studies do agree however, that in the post-exercise stretch, everyone is equal and should perform a thorough deep stretching routine to aid in muscle recovery, muscle soreness and injury prevention. Remember that any off court training program and stretching routine should be molded around your specific needs as an athlete. Try this routine that I begin and end each Futuremetrics session with:

- Start by rolling your neck around in each direction five times.
- Next reach both arms to the sky with your fingers laced together and hold for a 15 second count. (Repeat 3 times)
- Next, standing up, cross your left foot over your right and slowly bend down and touch the ground keeping your legs straight. Then switch your right foot over your left foot and do the same. (Repeat 3 times and hold all stretches for 10 seconds each time)
- Next push up against a wall at arms length with one foot slightly in front of the other. Keep the heel of the back foot on the ground as you lean forward straightening your back leg and stretching your calf muscle and Achilles tendon. Then switch legs and repeat 3 times.

- Next spread your legs out wide to the sides and then lean to the left and right stretching the groin area. (Hold each side for 10 seconds before switching)
- Next take a seat on the ground to stretch your hamstrings and lower back muscles. With both feet extended in front of you, reach down and try to see how far you can reach past your toes. This is a good test of your flexibility. Top athletes of various sports can reach well past their toes. (Repeat 3 times or as needed)
- Next sit with one leg straight out in front of you and then bend the other leg so that the bottom of your foot is up against your straightened leg. Reach forward over your foot. Switch and repeat 3 times.
- Finally, stand up on one leg and bend the other leg behind you grasping it with your hand. Pull upwards on your foot, pointing the knee to the ground and hold and balance for 10 seconds. Switch and repeat 3 times.
- Lightly jog in place for one minute.

Now you're ready!

Added stretches during exercise and for post-exercise stretching should include specific areas of muscle soreness, tightness or weakness.

| neckroll a | neckroll b | neckroll c |
| overhead stretch | left over right stretch | right over left stretch |

calf stretch

groin stretch

hamstring stretch

lowerback/ hams stretch

quad stretch

Self-Named Drills

These are explanations and photos of my self-named drills used in the Futuremetrics program.

Knee to Chest Walk

Walk twenty-five yards pulling your knee up towards your chest with each step.

knee ups

Jogging Ankle Kicks

Jog, kicking up your ankles behind you while leaning your upper body over your toes.

ankle-kicks

Forward step lunges

Step forward into a lunge so that the back leg knee goes to the ground and the front leg knee doesn't go past the toes of your front foot.

step lunges

Bleacher Toe-ups

Start with one foot on the first step of the bleacher and the other foot on the ground. Begin switching the position of each foot as fast as you can without ever putting full weight on the foot that is on the bleacher.

toe-ups

Bleacher Feet–ups

Start with one foot on the first bleacher step and one foot on the ground. Step onto the bleacher so that both feet are side by side. Step back down again and continue as fast as you can. This is a timed drill usually 45 seconds to 1 minute each round.

bleacher feet-ups

Leap frog Run with Medicine ball

Works best with three or more people. Begin jogging in a single file line with the person at the front of the line carrying a 10lbs. medicine ball. As you jog along pass the medicine ball to the person behind you by twisting your upper body and gently tossing the ball. When the person in the back of the line finally receives the ball they must then sprint to the front of the line and start the process all over again. This run is usually one mile long.

leap frog medicine ball run

Ice Skate lunge

Just like it sounds. When you're training at the beach, on a sand volleyball court or on a clay court this is one of my favorite leg strengthening drills. Without picking up your feet slide them out ahead of you one by one as far as you can lunge. Just as if you were ice-skating in central Park.

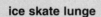

ice skate lunge

1st WEEK   Strength and Endurance
Goal—To build a player's overall body strength and increase cardiovascular endurance.

Monday

15-minute stretch routine
1.5 mile run under 20 minutes
25-yard knee to chest walk-5 times (continuous) then jog 5 times with walk back to start
25 yard jogging ankle kicks-5 times (continuous)
25 yard lunges- 5 times with walk back to start after each (continuous)
25 yard 2 feet jumps- 5 times with walk back to start after each (continuous)
45-second bleacher toe ups with 45-second rest after each-5 times
45 second bleacher feet ups with 45-second rest after each- 5 times
100 sit-ups in sets of 25 with 30-50 push-ups in sets of 10 alternating
Stretch routine again and cool down

Tuesday
15-minute stretch routine
1.5 mile run under 20 minutes (5 minute rest after with stretch)
25-yard knee to chest walk-5 times (continuous) then jog 5 times with walk back to start
25 yard jogging ankle kicks with walk back to start-5 times (continuous)
25 yard lunges- 5 times. Walk back to start after each one (continuous)
25 yard shuffles with crossover lunge at each end- 5 times (repeat 5 times as needed)
45 second bleacher toe ups- 3 times with 45 second rest after each
45 second bleacher both feet up – 3 times with 45 second rest after each
100 sit-ups in sets of 25 with no rest alternating to 30 push-ups in sets of 10
Stretch routine and cool down

Wednesday
15-minute stretch routine
1.5-mile leapfrog runs with 10lb. Medicine ball under 20 minutes (5 minute rest with stretch)
25-yard knee to chest walk-5 times (continuous)
25 yard jogging ankle kicks-5 times with walk back to start (continuous)
25 yard lunges- 3 times with walk back to start (continuous)
25 yard shuffles with crossover lunge at each end- 5 times continuous (Repeat 5 times)
25 yard right leg only hops with walk back to start- 5 times
25 yard left leg hops only with walk back to start- 5 times
minutes of forehand and backhand medicine ball toss
100 sit-ups and 50 push-ups in sets of 20 and 10 each with no rest (alternating)
Stretch and cool down

Thursday

15-minute stretch routine

1.5 mile run under 18 minutes (5 minute rest with stretch)

25-yard knee to chest walk-5 times (continuous) then jog 5 times with walk back to start

25 yard jogging ankle kicks-5 times with walk back to start (continuous)

25 yard shuffle drill with alternating crossover and side lunge on each end 5 times continuous (Repeat 5 Times)

25 yard lunges- 3 times with walk back to start (continuous)

25 yard sprints down and back with long jump at each end – Repeat 10 times (20 second Intervals)

50 push –ups in sets of 10 with 20 second rest after each set

Countdown Crunches- start with 30 then 20, 15, 10, 5 (crunches in 20 second intervals)

Stretch and cool down

Friday (Beach Day)

10-minute stretch

1.5 mile run to the beach or on the beach under 18 minutes (5 minute rest with stretch)

25-yard knee to chest walk in sand-5 times with walk back to start (continuous)

25-yard jogging ankle kicks in sand-5 times with walk back to start (continuous)

25 yard lunges in sand- 5 times with walk back to start (continuous)

25 yard ice skate in the sand- 5 times with walk back to start (continuous)

25-yard sprints with a long jump at the end- 5 times with walk back to start (20 second)

1.5 miles run back under 18 minutes

Stretch and cool down

Drills needed for week two:

Speed Obstacle course#1
Set up course from left to right:
30 foot rope laid out in a straight line
10 cones, set 3 heel-to-toe steps apart, perpendicular to the 30 foot rope 10 feet to the right of rope.
3 tennis balls, set 10 feet to the right of the cones, positioned at the end-side of the cones and rope.

Player starts in the center of the speed obstacle course, ten feet from the first cone. Going as fast as possible, the player hops over each cone putting down two steps in-between each cone. After going through the cones the player then skips over and back across the rope until reaching the end, then the player sprints around the stations to the tennis balls and picking up one ball at a time, does three 30 yard sprints to bring each ball back to the starting line. (Entire course is timed)(Beat 33 seconds)(10 rounds max)

Speed Obstacle course#2
Set up course from left to right:
30 foot rope laid out in a straight line.
10 cones, set 3 heel-to- toe steps apart, perpendicular to rope, 10 feet to the right of rope.
3 tennis balls, set 10 feet to the right of cones, positioned at the end-side of the cones and rope.

The player again starts in the center of the obstacle course ten feet from the first cone. Going as fast as possible the player split steps at each cone then puts down two steps between each cone. After going through the cones the player jumps with two feet over and back across the rope until reaching the end, then the player sprints around the stations to the tennis balls and picking up one ball at a time does three 30 yard sprints to bring each ball back to the starting line. (Entire course is timed)(Beat 18 seconds)(8 rounds)

Strength and speed course#1

Set up 8 cones in a zigzag pattern 10 yards apart across a field or tennis courts.
Player sprints to each cone and simulates hitting a low closed stance forehand when going to the right and a low closed stance backhand when going to the left. This is a timed course.

Strength and speed course#2

Set up 8 cones in a zigzag pattern 15-20 yards apart across a field or a bank of tennis courts.
Player sprints to each cone and then does 5 grasshoppers. A grasshopper is when you drop from a standing position and into a push-up position and then back up to a standing position where you then jump and reach both arms to the sky. This is a timed course.

Sand Tag

This great if you have three or more people. Mark off a large square in the sand. Everyone is inside the square and one person is trying to tag all the rest. Your job is not to get tag. When you do get tagged you step out of the square. To make it harder for the person trying to tag, make the square bigger and for making it harder for those trying not to get tagged, make the square smaller.

2nd WEEK Strength and Speed
Goal—To continue increasing overall body strength while adding speed in short distances.

<u>Monday</u>
15-minute stretch
1.5 mile run under 20 minutes (5 minute rest/stretch)
25-yard two feet jumps-3 times with walk back to start (continuous)
25 yard Left foot only jumps-3 times with walk back to start (continuous)
25 yard right foot only jumps- 3 times with walk back to start (continuous)
Sprinters test—Do the first four test, 3 times each. (see chapter one- page 16)
50 yard sprints- 10 times with jog back to start (continuous)
Speed obstacle course#1- 10 times (timed under 33 seconds)
100 sit ups and 30 push ups alternating in sets of 25 and 10
Stretch and cool down

<u>Tuesday</u>
15-minute stretch
1.5 mile run under 20 minutes (5 minute rest/stretch)
25-yard knee to chest walk-5 times with walk back to start (continuous)
25 yard sprints-5 times with walk back to start (under 4 seconds)
25 yard ice skate lunges- 4 times with walk back to start (continuous)
Speed obstacle course#2- 10 times
100 sit ups and 40 push ups in sets of 25 and 10
Stretch and cool down

<u>Wednesday</u>
15-minute stretch
1.5-mile leapfrog run with 10lb. Medicine ball under 25 minutes (5 minute rest/stretch)
25-yard knee to chest walk-5 times (continuous) then jog 5 times continuous
25 yard jogging ankle kicks-5 times with walk back to start (continuous)
50 yard sprints- 8 times with walk back to start (under 10 seconds)

Strength and Speed course#1 10 times
minutes of forehand and backhand medicine ball toss or 50 each side
100 sit-ups and 50 push-ups in sets of 20 and 10 alternating with no rest
Stretch and cool down

Thursday
15-minute stretch
1.5 mile run under 18 minutes (5 minute rest/stretch)
25-yard knee to chest walk-5 times (continuous) then Jog 5 times (continuous)
25 yard jogging ankle kicks-5 times with walk back to start (continuous)
Sprinters Test—first 4 test –3 times each (page 16)
Strength and Speed course#2 8 times
60 push-ups or medicine ball throws from the knees 60 each side in sets of 10 (20 second rest between sets)
Crunch countdown—30, 25, 20, 15, 10, 5 crunches (20 second intervals)
Stretch and cool down

Friday (Beach Day)
10-minute stretch
1.5 mile run to the beach or on the beach under 18 minutes (5 minute rest/stretch)
25-yard knee to chest walk in sand-5 times with walk back to start (continuous)
25-yard jogging ankle kicks in sand-5 times with walk back to start (continuous)
Sand tag 10 minutes or 5 tags by each person (mark off a big square and play tag within)
25 yard ice skate in the sand- 5 times with walk back to start (continuous)
25-yard sprints with long jump- 5 times with walk back to start (20 sec. Intervals)
1.5 miles run back under 18 minutes
Stretch and cool down

Power and Agility Course (3rd week)

Set up circular course in this order:

Hexagon jumps-jump in and out of hexagon going across each side. (3 times around)

Jump rope station—15 one leg jumps each leg.

10-10lbs. Medicine ball overhead throws. —Using a wall or pole have player touch the back of their neck and then throw as high as they can on the wall.

10 cones 2-step with shuffle return—3 times through—set up 10 cones 3 heel to toe steps apart. Player hops through putting down two steps between each cone and then side shuffling back to start.

35 feet—5-line suicide sprint or shuffle. (Each line 7ft apart)

Player starts at hexagon station then moves to the jump rope station, then to the medicine ball station, then to the cone station, then to the sprint station. Player goes through the entire course while being timed. Player tries to improve time each session the course is used.

(See Drill Pages)

Wheel Run

Set up four cones in a 36 foot square. Put one cone in the direct center. Player runs to center cone and then out to a corner cone until all four cones have been touched and player returns to start. (Timed under 16 seconds)
(See Drill pages)

3rd WEEK Power and Agility
Goal—To use newly added strength and speed to generate power, while continuing focus on short distant movement and recovery.

Monday
15-minute stretch
Half mile run under 8 minutes (5 minute rest/stretch)
25-yard knee to chest walk-5 times (continuous) then jog 5 times with walk back to start
25 yard jogging ankle kicks-5 times with walk back to start
50 yard sprints- 5 times (20 second intervals)
100 yard sprints- 5 times (20 second intervals)
Power and Agility course—7 times
Stretch and cool down

Tuesday
15-minute stretch
Half mile run under 8 minutes (5 minute rest/stretch)
25-yard knee to chest walk-5 times (continuous) then jog 5 times with walk back to start
25 yard shuffles with crossover lunge at each end- 5 times down and back (Repeat 5)
100 yard sprints—5 times with walk back to start
50 yard 3 foot leaps—5 times with walk back to start
25 yard sprints—5 times with walk back to start
Power and Agility course—5 times
100 set ups with 30 push ups alternating in sets of 25 and 10
Stretch and cool down

Wednesday
15-minute stretch
1.5-mile leapfrog runs with 10lb. Medicine ball under 25 minutes (5 minute rest/stretch)
minutes of forehand and backhand medicine ball toss to partner from knees

Power and Agility course—8 times
100 sit-ups and 50 push-ups in sets of 20 and 10 alternating with no rest
Stretch and cool down

Thursday
15-minute stretch
Half mile run under 8 minutes (5 minute rest/stretch)
25 yard knee to chest walk (continuous)
7 Wheel Runs with 30 seconds rest after each
25 yard sprints with long jump at each end- 10 times (20 second Intervals)
Power and Agility course—4 times
50 push-ups in sets of 10 with 20 second rest between each set.
Crunch countdown—30, 15, 10, 10, 5 crunches (20 second intervals)
Stretch and cool down

Friday (Beach Day)
10-minute stretch
1.5 mile run to the beach or on the beach under 18 minutes (5 minute rest/stretch)
25-yard knee to chest walk in sand-5 times with walk back to start (continuous)
25-yard jogging ankle kicks in sand-5 times with walk back to start (continuous)
Sand Tag- 10 minutes (continuous)
25 yard ice skate in the sand- 5 times with walk back to start (continuous)
25-yard sprints with long jump- 5 times (20 sec. Intervals)
1.5 miles run back under 18 minutes
Stretch and cool down

Speed and Agility Course (for 4th week)
Set up circular course in this order:
Hexagon jumps-jump in and out of hexagon going across each side. (3 times around timed)
Jump rope station—50 running in place jumps.
20-yard sprint with a jump over a cone at the end and then a catch of a ball tossed to right or left.

10 cones 2-step with shuffle return—3 times through—set up 10 cones 3 heels to toe steps apart. Player hops through putting down two steps between each cone and then side shuffling back to start.
35 feet 5-line suicide sprint. (Each line 7ft apart)

Player starts at the hexagon station, and then moves to the jump rope station, then to the 20-yard sprint station, then to the cone station, then to the sprint station. Player goes through the entire course while being timed. Player tries to improve time each session the course is used.

2 Cone sprint and Shuffle

Put 2 cones in the middle of the baseline exactly 3 yards apart. Player starts at the right doubles sideline and sprints to the first cone, then does a crossover step over the cone and shuffles to the next cone and does another crossover step and then sprints to the other sideline and then comes back through the course. (Repeat twice under 20 seconds)(See drill Pages)

Frisbee Sprints
Place 10 cones in a zigzag pattern about 3 feet apart. Players must sprint and shuffle through and around all 10 cones. Once through the cones the coach throws a Frisbee out to the left or right side and the player must chase it down and make the catch. This is great for agility because of how the Frisbee changes directions in the air forcing the player to mimic the directional change with their feet.

4th WEEK Speed, Quickness and Reflex
Goal—To increase reaction time, maximum running velocity and explosive power within short and long distances.

Monday
15-minute stretch

1-mile sprint/walk/ jog—Timed for 20 minutes (change pace every 220) (5minute rest/stretch)

25-yard knee to chest walk-5 times with walk back to start then jog 5 times

45-second bleacher feet with 45-second rest-5 times

45 second bleacher both feet up with 45-second rest- 5 times

Suicide Sprints 3 times under 30-seconds each (use the lines of a tennis court)

Suicide Shuffles 3 times (timed less than 45 seconds each)

The Wheel Drill 5 times (timed less than 30 seconds)

Typewriter feet with jump and shuffle 90 seconds (5 times)

Stretch and cool down

Tuesday
15-minute stretch

1-mile sprint/walk/jog—Timed 20 minutes (2 minute rest)(change pace every 110)

5 minute rest/Stretch

25-yard knee to chest walk-5 times with walk back to start (continuous)

45 second bleacher toe ups- 3 times with 30 second rest between

45 second bleacher both feet up – 3 times with 30 second rest between

Speed and Agility Course— 7 times

Typewriter feet with sky jumps only—5 times 30 seconds (stamp feet as fast as possible)

100 sit –ups 40 push-ups in sets of 25 and 10 alternating with no rest.

Stretch and cool down

Wednesday
15-minute stretch
1.5-mile leapfrog runs with 10lb. Medicine ball under 20 minutes
5 minutes rest/stretch
25-yard knee to chest walk-5 times with walk back to start (continuous) then jog 5 times
Speed and agility course—7 times
Frisbee Sprints (10 times)
100 sit-ups and 50 push-ups in sets of 20 and 10 alternating with no rest
Stretch and cool down

Thursday
15-minute stretch
1-mile sprint/walk/jog—Timed 18 minutes (pace is 220 for jog & sprint, 110 for walk)(5 minute rest stretch)
25-yard knee to chest walk-5 times with walk back to start (continuous)
25 yard jogging ankle kicks-5 times with walk back to start after each
Speed and Agility course— 5 times
Frisbee Sprints (10 times)
2 cone sprint and shuffle—7 times (Timed twice through under 20 seconds)
Stretch and cool down

Friday (Beach Day)
minute stretch
1.5 mile run to the beach or on the beach under 14 minutes (5 minute rest/stretch)
25-yard knee to chest walk in sand-5 times with walk back to start (continuous)
25-yard jogging ankle kicks in sand-5 times with walk back to start (continuous)
25 yard ice skate in the sand- 5 times with walk back to start (continuous)
Frisbee Sprints 10 times
1 mile sprint/walk/jog on the beach changing every 110.
Stretch and cool down

Training Note:

Once you have completed a four-week session access your fitness level before starting the next four-week session. If your fitness level is in the above average range, increase each week by ten to twenty percent by either increasing the number of times you do each drill or by decreasing the amount of rest between rounds or sets. Also cut back to a three days a week maintenance program using Futuremetrics days Monday, Wednesday and Friday of each specific week as your guide. You should design your Futuremetrics program to fit your specific needs. For example, if your endurance level is high but you are still weak in the power or strength areas then put more focus into these areas until you have equaled your endurance level and vise-versa. Coaches, look to add new drills that have similar results, every four weeks to keep the training program fresh and fun.

As with any conditioning program don't forget to add in days of rest to avoid over training. Intense training without proper rest can lead to injury and or illness. Here are some signs of over training that you should be aware of:

Consistent muscle soreness—It's natural to be sore as you go through the first four weeks of a Futuremetrics program or any conditioning program for that fact, as you are building up muscle strength. But persistent muscle soreness is not good and should be treated as signal to back off or retool your program.

Sleepless nights—If you're having trouble sleeping through the night then your muscles are over worked.

Not hungry or see a dramatic weight loss.

Mood swings—If you're more irritable anxious or unmotivated.

Getting sick too often is a sign of possible over training.

Dizzy spells or light headiness.

When you are showing signs of over training the answer is rest. Take a few days off and rest. If you feel the need to workout try something different like swimming, surfing or a bike riding. A few days away from intense training can do wonders for you both physically and mentally.

If you are an active tournament player, your conditioning program schedule should be scaled down to consider the on court grind. A competitive player's Futuremetrics schedule would look something like this:

Weekly

Strength training of key muscle groups, 3 times a week—during tournament weeks keep the intensity high but the number of reps low. When not a tournament week go with low intensity and high reps.

Endurance training 2 times a week—distant running 20-30 minutes or bike ride.

Speed and quickness training—you'll get a lot of this on the court so 2 times a week should be fine. Sprint work like, suicide sprints and shuffles for speed and jump rope for quick feet is always good.

Flexibility—a stretching routine should be performed daily.

The Future of Futuremetrics

Futuremetrics has recently been overhauled. We have added left-side brain stimulators into a lot of the Futuremetrics drills in order to bring out more creativity and better problem solving in our players during their on court performances.

In any sport or physical activity you are involved in, it is your right side brain that is stimulated during performance, which aids in helping you to perform physically all the required motor skills. The left side brain is not stimulated as it is used more in the creative and problem solving areas of sport and life. People like: artist, musicians, writers and all those who create are very left side brain orientated. When an athlete comes along who not only physically performs well but who also problem solves or is very creative in his or her performance well, then you have someone very special. (For example: Martina Hingis, Tiger Woods, Serena Williams, Julius Erving, Annika Sorenstam) Tennis is definitely a sport that has room for creating during play as does sports like golf and basketball just to name a couple.

The idea, adding brain stimulators to the Futuremetrics drills, is to increase a player's ability to think better and make better decisions even when physically exhausted or under extreme physical stress. How? By having them do some sort of creating or problem solving during strenuous off court physical exercises so that the left side brain is as stimulated as the right side brain therefore enhancing the players ability to think and prob-

lem solve his or her way through highly strenuous and competitive point, game and match situations.

To do this I have created note cards, paper size and poster size sheets filled with puzzles, riddles, mathematical problems, shot combinations, fill in the blanks, ink blots and a variety of other mind bending brain stimulators that I now use in specific drills of each Futuremetrics training session. How does it actually work, you ask?

As a player in the Futuremetrics program is strenuously doing an exercise or drill, for example a set of 50 sit ups or a set of bleacher toe-ups, a poster is shown or a note card flashed with a problem on it and the player must figure out the answer to the problem, which could be in the form of a question, riddle or puzzle, in the required time. If the answer isn't given after a certain time then a new card is shown to create new brain stimulation. Another example is, have a player do ten sprints with 20 second rest intervals and flash time tables or simple geometric puzzles to them to answer during the 20 seconds of rest, then send them off again on the next sprint. The key is to stimulate quickly within the exercise while performing or when exhausted. You can use pictures with quick true or false questions on them or simple fill in the blank questions. When the player starts answering the questions quicker or solving the puzzles and problems better then it is time to take it to the tennis courts and see if that same player can make quicker, better decisions within a point, during a game and throughout a match.

These problem solving brain stimulators also add the key ingredient of fun into any off court training session and you may find there is more laughter then groans in your next sessions. Remember tennis is a sport that has room for both right-side and left-side brain stimulation during play.

A few more Examples:
• While riding a stationary bike, the player solves complex puzzles, mathematical problems or does tennis crosswords.
• While jumping on and off of a plyometric box or doing bleacher feet ups, the player must react to visual commands that represent stop, go, jump to the left and jump to the right. These visual commands can be your hand or a tennis racquet.
• After completing an obstacle course run, players must quickly solve jumbled word puzzles or phrases.

• After a suicide run or shuffle, players must solve picture puzzles on poster boards that have one picture that doesn't belong. Example: duck, parrot, sparrow, cow. Obviously cow does not belong, as the rest are birds.

• Set up 30 cones in a scattered pattern with 10 colored balls under ten of the cones. Make sure to have 5 matching pairs. Players do sprints or suicides that end at the cones. A player can pick up one cone and if there is a colored ball beneath it then after the next sprint that player gets one pick to match the colored ball. If no match then the cones are replaced over the balls and the player must remember the placement.

In order to get one sprint taken off all players are asked a riddle like: What animal can jump higher then a house? Answer: all animals because houses can't jump.

COACHES NOTE: Mind stimulators do not have to be difficult. Remember to Keep it Simple and fun but always have a mind eraser in your back pocket for those days when your players get a little too full of themselves.

Jim Courier

What Jim Courier lacked in natural talent he made up for tenfold in his physical fitness. Courier was a working mans player who took a game full of unorthodox strokes and shots and molded them around superior footwork, physical fitness and mental toughness. Courier used to take a lot of pride in dismantling opponents with his heavy powerful groundstrokes in tournaments played in the most extreme conditions that required, not just great ball striking to win, but also endurance, power and perseverance.

Courier set new standards for tennis players in fitness and training. They used to call Jim Courier 'Rock' when he was playing because of his superior fitness level. As the story goes a player accidentally ran into Jim one day in a hallway and told everyone it felt like he had run into a rock wall, other players agreed and so the nickname stuck.

Jim courier won four Grand Slam titles: two Australian Open titles and two French Open titles. He was the #1 player in the world in 1992-93.

Top Five Fitness Training Tips

1. Push yourself hard everyday
2. Never say "I can't."
3. Accept the challenge to better your previous times
4. Make consistency a habit
5. Enjoy the self-confidence that comes with feeling stronger, faster and fitter.

Coach's Notebook:

Early Ages (5-9)—It's never too early to begin working on your footwork, racquet speed, quickness, flexibility and reflexes. But when it comes to strength training with weights you must wait until the young player's body is more developed as to not hinder the natural growing process. Running, jumping and reacting are all part of a kids life and should be encouraged through alternate sports. I can't stress enough the benefits a player receives athletically by playing or just practicing a variety of other sports at an early age.

Jr Tournament Level Player—If your body is developed then you should start a full Futuremetrics style-conditioning program that includes strength training. If you are still growing you may want to put extra time into the speed and agility portions of the program so that your footwork stays ahead of your body growth. I see a lot of clumsy footed players at this stage that could greatly improve their performance if they would spend a half hour a day just doing footwork drills. Make flexibility and core strength a constant goal. Also it's time to discipline yourself as well as your game and for that reason I suggest you do your conditioning program at 6am every morning. Why? Because if you can discipline yourself to get up out of bed everyday to do the hard work then you'll be able to discipline your game and everything around your game as well. Sorry parents and coaches.

Pro Player Beginnings—Fitness should be a way of life for you at this stage. You should design your conditioning program around your tournament schedule and according to your specific needs. If you're in the slow clay court season you may have a need for better endurance and so adding some more long distance runs into your weekly routine may be the answer. If you're coming into the hard court season you may find you need more strength and power and might want to add more reps or more weight into your routine. What ever your specific needs are at the time are what should dictate your Futuremetrics drills and off-court conditioning program overall. The important thing is that you are doing something everyday to better your physical needs and athletic skills. Maintain flexibility and core strength as constant goals.

CHAPTER NINE

TACTICS AND STRATEGY

When it comes to tactics and strategies (your game plan), you must remember that the score matters. It matters because it depicts the amount of risk you can take on your shot. Taking the proper amount of risk, according to your skills, the skills of the opponent, based on the pressure of the situation is what having a good tactical game plan is all about.

Today's game plans require shots of greater risk than were once used before, because of the fact that nowadays players have the ability to hit winners from any position on the court. When there is an opening you must be able to take advantage of it and if there is not an opening then you need to be able to create one. Don't be afraid to take risks within your game plan. I often remind my players to take at least one risk per point no matter what the score, and when the score is in their favor then they can take multiple risks. You must of course; own the shot of risk you are trying to attempt and often you will need to be patient and consistent until you get to that shot of risk. Being prepared mentally as well as physically to hit the shot of risk when it appears within your crosscourt based game plan though

is what matters most. **Early preparation is a key fundamental.**

Crosscourt Based Game Plan

A solid game plan of the New Game consists of a crosscourt base with frequent shots of risk. By crosscourt base I mean that you must have the ability to hit your strokes and shots crosscourt at any time throughout a rally. At times when you are put on defense and you need to use more court to hit a deep penetrating shot, at times when your opponent hits a short ball and you want to open up the court with the angle and at times when you want to use the low part of the net to neutralize your opponent with a low setup shot or passing shot. Crosscourt should be your base and you need to practice consistently hitting all your strokes and shots there daily. Here are some drills that will help you to establish a crosscourt-based game.

Top Five Drills for developing a crosscourt based game

1. Crosscourt-down-the-line drill—This is a classic drill used by just about every high level tournament player. A coach or practice partner hits all balls crosscourt with consistency while the player hits down the line flat with authority. Then switch and repeat.

2. Hit everything crosscourt drill—Coach or practice partner hits a variety of shots to all areas of the court while the player focuses on only hitting crosscourt shots within the rally.

3. Passing crosscourt drill—Have a coach or practice partner hit different style approach shots at you so that you can practice hitting crosscourt passing shots. Play to 10 points.

4. Crosscourt angles drill—Two players stand in opposite crosscourt corners and rally. The players try not to make mistakes while trying to hit angled shots that land inside the service line. For every shot inside the service line you get one point.

5. Return crosscourt drill—Coach or practice partner hits different types of serves. You must return all serves crosscourt to start the point. Try for more angles on wide serves and high bouncing flat serves.

(See drill pages for more on drills # 1 & 2)

Shots of risk and reward should be selected out of this crosscourt-based game plan based on a few different factors. The main factor of course is do you own the shot you are trying to hit. Next is where is your opponent and does he or she have a weakness and finally what is the score situation.

Situations

As a player you can't start practicing actual game situations too soon. In fact as soon as you are able to serve and keep score you should begin to learn how to react under the pressures of the score as well as those pressures applied by your opponent.

This becomes a key area that separates the pretenders from the true contenders and the teachers from the coaches. If you're still in the developing stages of your game then yes learning all the shots is very important but if you're already somewhat of a skilled ball striker and shot maker yet you're still getting your practices primarily from a coach feeding balls from a ball basket then I suggest you re-evaluate your goals, practice plans and your coach. I'll start practicing situations with players as young as six years old if I see that their stroke and shot making development is on course because I want that player to become accustom to the pressure of the score as early as possible before the experience layers get too thick.

It's important that you practice every situation possible and then be able to transfer what is learned on the practice court into your match play. I'm sure all of you have practiced situations at some point in your life. Think back, I'm sure you did. Did you ever go to the courts with a friend on a Sunday afternoon and say, "OK, I'll be Pete and you be Andre or I'll be Venus and you're Serena and this is the finals of the US Open." Well if you did that then you were practicing a situation. You were making the match more important then just a Sunday afternoon match and putting a lot more pressure on yourself to have a favorable outcome, in this case win the US Open. That's situational practicing, adding importance and pressure to points, games, sets or matches.

Every point in a game, set and match is important and your ultimate goal is to win every one. Ah, the **Golden Set**. But there are certain points within games and certain points within the match that are more important. Let's take a look at my top five point situations within games first.

Top Five Point Situations

1. **Score is tied: 30-30 or Deuce**
2. **You are two points ahead: 30-0, 40-15 serving or 0-30, 15-40 receiving**
3. **You are two points behind: 0-30, 15-40 serving or 30-0, 40-15 receiving**
4. **You are one point behind: 15-30, 30-40 serving or 30-15, 40-30 receiving**
5. **You are one point ahead: 30-15, 40-30 serving or 15-30, 30-40 receiving**

The Score is Tied

Deuce or 30-30 is a situation that requires a combination of every offensive, neutralizing and defensive shot you've learned. Your first job in this situation is to Get Two! By that I mean you must make your first two shots. Either a serve and the next ball or a return and the next ball. When you do this you are saying to your opponent that you are not going to give away these points for free. They are going to have to be earned points and you are willing to earn them each time. After you make two shots then you should begin looking for your favorite winning shot combinations or winning shots out of your crosscourt based game plan to end the point.

Player Note: For deuce and all situations you should have your own personal top five ways you like to win points. For example: If your forehand is your favorite weapon and the inside out forehand is one of your top five favorite winning shots, then you should hit set up shots that open up that zone of the court and that entice your opponent to hit balls down the middle of the court so you can run around them and hit inside out forehands. Set up shots like a deep crosscourt shot to the forehand or a deep down the line shot to the backhand might get you a response to the middle of the court.

Set Up Shots

Any shot that gets your opponent to hit you your favorite winning shots is considered a set up shot. If it's your backhand down the line that is one of your favorite winning shots then you should hit the inside out forehand as a set up shot to get a crosscourt response so that you can hit your backhand down the line. Other shots to set you up for the down the line backhands are: backhand angles, forehands down the line and deep balls to the opponents' backhands.

The key is that you know which shots you like to win points hitting and that you hit the proper set up shots to increase your chances of getting opportunities to hit those winning shots. You can't just be out on the court hitting balls back over the net with no purpose, no matter how hard or how accurate you are hitting, because today's players don't make easy unforced errors. That's why you need to have a solid game plan so that you can force an error from your opponent or hit a winner. A good rule to live by is: 93% of all your shots need to be hit with a purpose if you want to be 100% successful.

Up Two Points

Now say you are ahead by two points either 40-15 serving or 0-30 returning. You now have the green light to hit any of your winning shots at anytime during the point. Sharp flat angles, drop shots, down the line missiles anything that doesn't say conservative, safe or careful on it. Try that serve and volley combination you've been working on in practice or that chip and charge move with a drop volley finisher. The key in this situation is that you be aggressive from the start of the point, for two reasons; 1. To help your own confidence in using aggressive shots more often in your matches and 2. To send a message to your opponent that you are here to win this match and you are going to do it by being aggressive. If you send out those messages early in a match then every time your opponent is two points down they are going to feel the pressure about hitting certain shots, which could result in errors.

Down Two Points

When the situation is reversed and you are the one down two points 15-40 serving or 30-0 returning its time to go back to your crosscourt based game where you can be more consistent and play better defense. There aren't many times when you'll hear me tell my players to think defense but this situation is one that requires you to grind, dig and do whatever it takes to win that point in order to stay in the game. If you can close the gap to one point then pressure becomes a factor again for your opponent, especially to a serving

opponent, and opportunities will once again present themselves. It's no time to be thinking about hitting a quick winner and it is time to let your opponent lose the point by making an error.

Player Note: Did you realize that you do not have to win or lose every point yourself? You can let your opponent make some errors and lose some points also. Remember, this is a game of mistakes. I do know players however that just aren't happy unless they hit all winners on every point. Know this; those players never win big tournaments. Why? Because to win big tournaments you have to win seven rounds and nobody can win seven rounds all on their own shots. It takes a good amount of winners that's for sure but it also takes a lot of mistakes from your opponents and then it takes a little luck. And in order to let your opponent make mistakes you need to be able to stay in the point with a consistent crosscourt-based game plan.

Down One Point

When you are down one point, 30-40 serving or 40-30 returning, be consistent, but use the point previously played to gage your plan of attack. Before stepping up to serve or getting into position to receive think about what just happened and how you played the previous point. If you won the point by hitting a winner then you have the momentum going into this point and so you should try to play aggressively after getting the first ball in play. If you win this point also, then your back to a tie score and on a minnie run that could prove to be devastating for your opponent's confidence if it continues. If you lost the previous point by making an error then you must go back to your consistent crosscourt-based game to try and stop your opponent from gaining double momentum by winning another consecutive point and the game. Tennis is a game that is played in the present and normally I would tell you to stay in the present and play the point at hand but in this case looking back one point is a good aid to help you in your strategy of the now.

Up One Point

When you are carrying the lead by one point, 40-30 serving or 30-40 returning, look to play a solid point. Again it's a good time to look back at the previous point to gage your plan of attack but even if you won the previous point don't lose your head and make a quick error. You want to play a solid point that consists of either a good first serve or return, then a set up shot of some sort that leads to one of your favorite winning shots. So why not go for a quick winner? Because tennis is a game that moves on momentum and finishes on confidence.

Player Note: Your job as a player is to build momentum through your match by executing shots and shot combinations that you've practiced for countless hours on the practice courts. As you win games by this display of solidly executed plays, you'll gain the confidence needed to win the match at hand. You can now take this newly gained confidence into your next match and try to build upon it. As you continue to play solid points your games will get easier and your matches shorter. There won't be as many momentum shifts because of erratic play and you'll find your percentages go up in the shot execution department. Remember you don't have to win every point yourself.

Other Big Point Situations

Set Points

Set Point UP—This is another time when you want to play a solid point that consists of a crosscourt base and maybe has one shot of risk. Take a moment before you serve or step into the receiving position and evaluate how you got to this situation. If you just hit two forehand winners then by all means try and set yourself up for another forehand. If your opponent has made a rash of unforced errors then you should go into your consistent crosscourt-based game and just wait. If you've been forcing the errors then by all means force again. By now you should have enough knowledge about your opponent's game to devise a one-point game plan to end the set. If you don't then you haven't done your job as player/coach taking in the knowledge of the match. Even if you do win this set you may lose the next two because of your lack of mental awareness of your opponent's game. If the set has been an even battle up to this point with both you and your opponent playing pressure points then, watch out. A set point means more

to your opponent then any deuce or game point and he or she will fight like a cornered dog with a bone not to give it up, so it may be time to throw in something a little different that your opponent wouldn't expect from you. Maybe it's a kick first serve to the backhand or a serve and volley or if returning a chip and charge. Whatever your one point game plan is, know this; this tactic will only work once per set and if your opponent is mentally alert then probably only once per match. If you don't feel comfortable straying outside your crosscourt-based game then don't. A quick error by you or an easy winner from your opponent is not going to help your cause. If you get to a second set point you may feel more confident trying it then but if you don't then stick to your crosscourt based game and grind.

Set Point DOWN—Now you are the one who is the cornered dog with the bone. It's time to use all those layers of mental toughness you've accumulated on your game to get out of this situation. If serving, the worst thing you could do here is double fault, so don't even put yourself in that situation. Make your first serve. Add some spin to your serve and then get down and ready to play the longest smartest point of the match. Reassure yourself that whatever your opponent throws at you will not be a problem. If you're feeling anxious or nervous take a trip to the back fence and clear yourself of all emotions and negative thoughts. Try and play a crosscourt-based point, keeping the point to your opponent's weaker side if there is one and keeping on the alert for any attempt at an out of the ordinary winner from your opponent who might get anxious and try to end the point. When you do win this point know that you just added another layer of mental toughness to your game and build upon that momentum to win that game and eventually the match.

Player Note-The 17th Box: If you're receiving in this situation, then the worst error you can make is to hit the ball into the 17th box. What's the 17th box you ask? It's the net's bottom square box at the center strap. Probably one of the worst shots a high-level player can hit because it has absolutely no chance of clearing the net even at its lowest point. When an opponent hits a ball into the 17th box remember what shot you just hit them and try and repeat that shot throughout the match. It could be a shot they don't like as much as it being the pressure of the situation that caused them to hit such a poor shot.

All my players know about the 17th box because at anytime during a practice if they hit the 17th box then they have to run one suicide sprint after practice. To add the key ingredient of fun into our practice, any 17th box shot can be cancelled by a net chord shot that rolls over and inside the lines. As practice is coming to a close it's always fun to see them intentionally trying to clip the top of the net with all their shots to get out of running any sprints.

Match Points

Match Point UP—As you step up to serve or receive at match point up, there is only one question to ask yourself, are you ready to win? Have you evolved enough as a player to handle all that goes along with success? Because with winning comes expectations. Expectations from yourself as well as from everyone around you. If it's a top player you are about to beat or the championship you are about to win then the expectations of your talent will be even greater once you have victory. If your answer is yes then you are ready, so let's put the finishing strategies into your game plan.

Take a moment again to reflect on how you got to this match point. There have obviously been certain first serves that have been working for you or you wouldn't have a match point, use one of those serves now. If you don't think you can make one of those serves due to the pressure of the situation then try and hit a serve that will set up your big forehand or big backhand. Try to end the point on your terms and never hope for an error from your opponent. Your attitude should be that you want the ball to come over the net so you can show your wares or force the error from your opponent one last time. If it's been a dogfight up to this point, try and out think your opponent and give them something that they're not expecting. Now that doesn't mean trying to hit a drop shot that has so much spin on it that it bounces back onto your side after crossing the net. What it does mean is that you might want to try a shot combination or pattern that you haven't shown in awhile but it must be something you are capable of doing. You need to know your limits, hit shots and shot combinations that you own and play within your crosscourt based game plan one more time to end this match.

If you are receiving then know this: if you get the return of serve back over the net and in play then all the pressure goes to your opponent, the server, for the rest of that point. Why? Because as everyone, including the server, knows, the server is suppose to hold serve, the server is suppose to have the advantage and the server is suppose to control the point. So go ahead and return aggressively but take away some of the risks by returning the serve right back at the server. If it's a deep enough return or the server doesn't move their feet then you'll force an error right away or set yourself up for a short ball winner. By hitting down the center you'll also take away any angle opportunities and force the server to play back to your baseline and you'll also be hitting over the lowest part of the net reducing your chances of making an error in the net. Return aggressively if you get a second serve. Your opponent won't want to double fault the match away so move in and look for a ball with less kick than normal or a soft slice. If there's any depth at all on your return then you should look to close in towards the net.

Match point DOWN—This is a situation like no other. You'll need to have the heart of the Tin Man, the brains of the Scarecrow, and the courage of the Lion and the mental toughness of every past champion to get out of this situation. This is when you will see a champion like Pete Sampras hit an ace or Andre Agassi rip a return winner or Venus Williams chase down a ball thought to be ungettable and hit a winner. Time and time again these champions come up with the big shots when they're match point down and this is when you need to be able to call upon your big shots to get you out of trouble too. It's no good to have an arsenal of big shots if you can only use them when there's no pressure.

If you're serving look back at the point you just played. Was your serve effective? If so use it again or use that serving momentum from the last point and try and serve an ace. If you lost the last point or missed your first serve then just go for placement. Try to serve to your opponent's weaker side if there is one but with a type of spin that you haven't used in a while. Then be ready for a long grinding point or a quick attack from your opponent. Some players get anxious at match point and get out of their winning routines and try to end the match with a couple of fast shots, so be on alert and ready to play defense. Don't let someone who never comes to the net bluff his or her way to victory by rushing the net off the return or coming in randomly during the point. Stay calm and hit your passing shot and remember it's just a bluff. They are playing the odds that you'll panic and make an error and they'll not even have to play a final shot.

If you're receiving get low and get a hockey goalie mentality, nothing is going to get by you. If it's a good serve hit your return over the low part of the net either right back at the server or crosscourt. If the serve enters your big shot zone then you must be ready to execute it. Think of all those practices where you worked on ripping returns to every part of the court and then take that attitude and step up and do it. There will still be a pressure change to the server if you get that return back over the net so that is still your main concern. Watch out for the player who tries to hit a first serve twice. If the first serve is closely missed don't move up too aggressively inside the baseline. You'll want to get the best look you can at the second serve and not have to short hop the ball if the server decides to go for it. Once the return is in play go to your crosscourt base and grind.

Player Note: Know this; for every match point you save in a match you add twice as many layers of mental toughness to your game. And if you end up winning the match after being match point down, you'll increase your confidence in how to win tough matches and maybe even send your once worthy opponent to the mental hospital.

Basic Tactical Baseline Shot Combinations & Winners

Out of your crosscourt based game plan you should be looking to execute your favorite shot combinations and favorite winning shots. Shot combinations are the tactical use of two or three shots to win a point. Any more then three shots used and you are using patterns and any less then two shots used and you are hitting winning shots. (All combinations and winning shots are right-hander vs. right-hander)

Winning Shots:

Action (Opponent)	Winning Response (You)
Crosscourt deep	Crosscourt rolled angle
Crosscourt short topspin	Flat Down the Line (DTL)
DTL deep	Crosscourt deep
DTL short	Crosscourt angle
Down the middle deep	Deep crosscourt or inside out deep
Down the middle short	Inside out angles or crosscourt angles

NOTE: (All winners above are for either forehand or backhand first action shots)
(Shot abbreviations: DTL= down the line, FH= forehand, BKH= backhand)

Shot Combinations

Action (You)	Response (Opponent)	Action (you)
FH deep crosscourt	FH crosscourt short	FH flat down the line
FH angle topspin	FH flat DTL	BKH crosscourt topspin
BKH deep crosscourt	BKH crosscourt short	BKH flat DTL
BKH angle short	BKH (DTL)	FH crosscourt topspin
FH deep middle	FH inside out topspin	BKH flat DTL
FH deep DTL	KH rolled angle short	BKH topspin DTL
FH slice short DTL	BKH crosscourt deep	BKH topspin crosscourt
BKH deep DTL	FH rolled angle short	FH topspin DTL
BKH slice short DTL	FH topspin crosscourt deep	FH crosscourt deep
FH inside out short	BKH deep DTL	FH topspin angle
FH inside out deep	BKH short topspin DTL	FH flat angle
FH inside out deep angle	BKH crosscourt deep	BKH topspin DTL
FH inside out short angle	BKH short angle	BKH Flat or DTL slice

FH inside out short	BKH flat DTL	FH deep court cross angle
FH inside out deep	BKH middle deep	FH inside out angle
FH inside out short	BKH middle low short	FH topspin crosscourt
FH inside out deep angle	BKH middle short topspin	FH inside out fla

NOTE :(For BKH inside out combinations, change first action of FH to BKH, response to FH and final action to the opposite of what is listed)

Basic Attacking Shot Combinations & Winning shots

When under attack from your opponent it is imperative that you can respond with a winning shot most of the time. When you are the one attacking it is the quality and placement of your approach shot that determines your opponents probable response. Below are my favorite winning shots and combinations to add to your overall game plan.

Winning Shots

Action (opponent)	Winning Response (You)
FH deep approach DTL	BKH crosscourt short angle
FH short approach DTL	BKH crosscourt deep or DTL topspin
FH approach crosscourt deep	FH crosscourt rolled angle or flat DTL
FH short approach crosscourt	FH topspin DTL or flat DTL
FH approach middle	FH or BKH inside out short angle

NOTE:(For BKH approach shots change action to BKH and response to opposite listed)

Shot Combinations

Action (You)	Response (Opponent)	Action (You)
FH Approach DTL short	BKH low DTL	FH volley short crosscourt
FH approach DTL deep slice	BKH high crosscourt	BKH volley DTL

Action (You)	Response (Opponent)	Action (You)
FH approach DTL flat	BKH topspin low angle	BKH drop volley
FH approach DTL topspin	BKH middle into body	Volley deep crosscourt
FH approach crosscourt court short	FH flat DTL	BKH volley cross
FH approach crosscourt deep low	FH high crosscourt	FH volley DTL
FH approach crosscourt deep	FH low angle	FH drop volley
FH approach crosscourt deep	FH middle into body	Volley short angle

NOTE :(For all backhand approach shots change the first action to BKH, the response to opposite listed and the final action to opposite listed.)

Point Patterns

Point patterns are the use of more then three shots to win a point. The player who controls the point pattern is the offensive or action player and the player who is counterpunching and scrambling throughout the point is the defensive or response player. You want to be the player who controls the action of the point pattern (the fisherman) not the player who is being controlled (the fish).

It's very important to keep a player scrambling and under your control once you have gained the control of a point pattern by your offensive action and until you can end the point with one of your favorite winning shots. When you do this to an opponent, I say, you have them on the hook. Having an opponent on the hook is a phrase that means you are hitting penetrating, well placed shots that keep them under the control and unable to escape your action, much like when a fisherman has a fish on the line and although the fish struggles to break free the fisherman has it under his control. Andre Agassi is without a doubt a player who controls most of the points he plays and when he has a player on the hook they rarely escape.

Once you do have an opponent on the hook two factors becoming increasingly important: shot control and taking time away. Having control of your shots is how you can keep an opponent scrambling in response to your action. To do this you must have a variety of shots and be able to change the direction of the ball at any time during the point. By hitting controlled shots with various spins and ball flights to all areas of the court you can keep an opponent off the offensive action but having control over your shots won't necessarily win you the point. To win the point you must be able to end the point and to do that you will need to take time away from your opponent's recovery within the point by taking the ball early. Taking the ball early, either on the rise or by moving in to cut a ball off in the air, steals valuable time away from an opponent who is scrambling to recover back to protect an open court. Some players can chase balls down defensively all day long when on the hook and eventually can escape or force you to make the error. Don't let this happen! Be ready to move in and take a ball early even if it means abandoning your loop backswing and only using a wrist snap motion to hit the ball or if it means taking the ball out of the air with a block volley or swing volley motion. Remember, you want to be the player who controls the point action; you want to be the fisherman.

As you practice point patterns try to quicken the pace of the pattern by taking one or all of the shots in the pattern early. Here are some point patterns that you can practice to keep an opponent on the hook.

Top Five Point Patterns

Action (You hit),	Response (Playing partner hits)
1. All shots DTL flat or slice	1. All shots crosscourt with topspin
2. All shots crosscourt flat or slice	2. All shots DTL with heavy topspin
3. Mix shots changing direction of all short balls	3. All shots hit Crosscourt
4. Approach DTL, smash, volley,	4. Lob, groundstroke, lob...ECT. smash...ECT.
5. Approach crosscourt, hit volleys to one side	5. Mix in a variety of groundstrokes

NOTE: (Change each point pattern around so that you play as the action player and as the response player so that you know how to react to each side of the situation.)

❖ *The Venus & Serena Factor* ❖

Serena Williams

On the WTA tour, Serena is known to be the tougher of the Williams sisters to strategize against primarily because she has more shots and more weapons to choose from. You can't be a great tactician unless you have a wide range of shots and strokes at your disposal and Serena has them all.

Serena is known for her angles as well as her penetrating groundstrokes and she never over uses either, which makes her so hard to predict. There's not a shot she doesn't own and she accepts the challenge in each match to try and win points many different ways just to keep a player out of rhythm and without anticipation for her shots. When she was younger and she played me or another coach who had a shot that she didn't have, she would eagerly learn it and then practice on how to hit it as well as how to defend against it and then use it against me.

Serena makes it hard for an opponent to establish winning patterns or shot combinations because she is always mixing up her shot combinations and patterns. Every player knows that when Serena is down in a match she is not out of it. She will change her tactics immediately if they aren't working and she has never and will never give anyone a point for free.

In a practice match once I remember catching one of her mishaps that was clearly going long and out and do you know that she took the point from me reminding me that the rule states that I must let that ball bounce before calling it out. That unwillingness to give up a point is a key ingredient as to why she is the best woman player in the New Game.

A Little about Doubles Strategy and Tactics

Doubles brings the team aspect into this game of individuality. You can't be a successful doubles team if you and your partner are on the court playing your singles games. In other words forget about all the shot combinations and patterns you just learned because doubles has its own set of shots and strategies that you must learn. I will however stick to the basics as this book is geared more for your singles game, but keep in mind that playing more doubles will definitely help improve your singles game. Why? Because in doubles it's the placement of you're shot and not as much the power of your shot that is more important. And as you get better at placing your shots in doubles then you will undoubtedly get better at placing your shots in singles making you a more consistent shot maker. Also if you and your partner play an attacking style doubles game, and you should, then you will learn how to end points quickly and at the net. But let's stick to the basics. The first basic ingredients about doubles that you must know are the three doubles formations.

The Three Basic Doubles Formations

1. One player up and one player back formation
2. Both players up at net formation
3. Both players back at the baseline formation

| doubles 1 up 1 back | doubles 2 up | doubles 2 back |

Each of these formations can be successful if you and your partner know where the vulnerable spots on the court are to cover. In the one player up and one player back formation the vulnerable spots are the hole behind the net player and the short crosscourt angle in front of the baseline player. In the both players up formation the vulnerable spot is near the baseline in the back of the court. In the both players back formation the vulnerable spots are the two-frontcourt angles.

Although you can play effectively out of each of the three formations, your ultimate goal as a team should be to both be together at the net, to be the attacking team. From the net position you and your partner have the best court perspective and an increased area of court to use to hit to your opponents vulnerable spots.

If you play this attacking style of doubles though, you must end the points quickly once getting to the net because of the vulnerable back court that you will leave open. Your opponents can easily lob into this open area if given the additional shot opportunities and if you and your partner close in too close to the net you will not be able to cover the back.

The lob should not scare you from attacking the net though because even if the lob is the greatest threat to the attacking style team then the overhead smash is the perfect answer. In other words you must own a good overhead to play attacking style doubles. Teams that don't attack the net are usually protecting their weak volley or their inability to put the ball away with an overhead. If that's the case bring them to the net with short volleys and then finish them off with a volley right at their feet or over them. A true attacking team knows the value of hitting at an opponent's feet rather then trying to hit finesse shots around them.

Top Five Keys for Attacking Doubles Success

1. **Serves**
2. **Returns**
3. **Poaching**
4. **Controlling the Net**
5. **Teamwork**

Serves

A good server in doubles knows how to place their serve to set up their partner at the net or spin their serve to give themselves more time to get to the net. Your goal in doubles is not to see how many aces you can hit, although that would be great, but rather to neutralize your opponents return game with consistently well placed serves.

The serve down the middle should be used about 80% of the time because it limits the returnee's use of angles and gives your partner a chance at poaching the first ball. Be sure to serve down the middle with a variety of spins and speeds though to keep the returnee from grooving in on your serve. Also mix in the wide serves as well as serves into the body the other 20% of the time.

If you can't seem to hold your serve and you've been hitting it down the middle and into the body most of the time then it may be that your partner at the net is sleeping. It's a team effort to hold serve in doubles and the net player has the responsibility to poach all returns that are hit weakly through the middle of the court. To help your partner to get a feel for when to poach you and your partner may want to use signals to communicate exactly where you are serving and what they are doing. This signaling will aid in your net players ability to anticipate where the receiver's shot is going according to your serve.

Returns

I believe, the return is the shot that makes up great doubles teams. Why? Because a team that can consistently keep the returns low, crosscourt and away from the ready to poach net player puts added pressure on the server to do all of the work to win his or her serve. That consistent pressure eventually will not only break the server's advantage but also psychologically break apart the opposing team's spirit because the server will feel as if he or she isn't getting any help. The return has to be a quality return though landing consistently crosscourt at the service line/singles sideline area with either dipping topspin or skipping slice. The occasional down the line bullet return should be used once the crosscourt base has been established.

To effectively take the net away as an attacking team you must have your return low so that your opponent's first volley has to be hit up into your charging racquet. Don't try to hit outright winners on the return as your job is again to set up your partner for a poach or neutralize the serve so that you can take over the net before your opponents do.

An example of a set up return might be a topspin shot that dips at the charging server's feet and an example of a neutralizing shot might be a short no-pace slice that again falls at the server's feet. Either shot gives your partner at the net a chance to anticipate the next shot and poach it off.

Poaching

When you are at the net and your partner is not, you are the traffic director. Whatever you do in the front of the court your partner should do the opposite in the back of the court. If you decide to switch to the other side of the court during a rally then your partner must switch to the other side in the backcourt. And if your partner doesn't like it, then too bad, because it's not up to them. I tell my doubles teams all the time that if you want to be the traffic director then you better get to the net and ahead of your partner otherwise if you stay back then you must move according to your partner's movements.

If you are the one at the net then you should be looking for every opportunity to move through the middle of the court and cut balls off before they reach your partner in the backcourt. Making this move through the middle court is known as the poaching move. Poaching consistently in a match puts added pressure on your opponents to hit better-placed cross-court or down the line shots that will often lead to an increase in errors. It only takes two or three effective poaches early in a match to set the precedent and have your opponents second-guessing their shot selections.

Knowing when to poach is a feeling that is determined by three factors: your partners shot placement, your opponent's strengths and weaknesses and the score situation. You only need one of these factors to be in your favor to make that decision to poach a green light. And if you should fail in executing the volley once you have poached don't let that discourage you. Just keep at it and soon you will start to time your move to the ball better. If you back off after missing a few volleys, your opponents will know they don't have to worry about you poaching the rest of the match sending them a signal to start attacking.

Teamwork

No one person can win a doubles match, it takes two. While you and your partner may each posse different shot making skills the fact still remains that you and your partner each have to effectively serve and return serve to be successful together.

What makes up a good partnership often has little to do with what shots each player owns and has everything to do with how well you communicate with each other and strategize together. Knowing your partner's strengths and weaknesses will help you plan your attack or mount your defense. But remember that can change daily. For example if your partner's usually strong serve is not happening you may find it necessary to guard the alley better and avoid risky poaches. As long as the two of you talk about the mood of the match as well as each other then you will be able to plan or change your plan of attack to fit the situation. The worst thing you can do as a team is not communicate what is going on in the match. There is no I in the word team.

Controlling the Net

To be an attacking team you must be able to control the net. To do that you and your partner must make the commitment to each other to come to the net at every available opportunity. Any short serve or shot must be taken advantage of and used to get yourself to the net. If you and your partner both know that the other is always going to come to the net on a short shot then it will help in anticipating your poaches and covering any other front court zone.

Once together at the net, if your opponents are both up or in a one back one up formation, try and keep your shots low at their feet to force them to hit back up to you. It's much easier to hit a winner on a ball that is rising at the net as opposed to a sinking ball. Also make the commitment to cover your own lobs. This is very important in controlling the net

because it keeps you and your partner from avoiding the switch so that your only movement is backwards and forwards. To cover your own lobs you will need to be skilled in the stamp it overhead, the standing overhead and the scissor kick overhead. Teams that move into a both back formation are doing so because they are planning to lob you and your partner off the net. One or two overhead winners will quickly have them changing tactics. If they now try to pass you at the net use angle volleys and drop volleys to take advantage of the vulnerable frontcourt. After a few winners in the frontcourt be ready for another tactical change by your opponents. You are now controlling the match all because you and your partner are controlling the net.

Other Tips

Momentum

Teamwork is the name of the game in doubles but there is still often going to be one partner who has the momentum within the point, game or match. Be aware of when your partner is hitting a particularly great shot or shot combination and stay out of the way of those shots that are entering those zones. For example, during a set if your partner, on the deuce side, has been hitting unbelievable angles off of any shot hit to his or her forehand then by all means the rest of the set don't go chasing after balls that are hit in that direction. Let your partner build his or her confidence upon the execution of that forehand shot and set you up for easy winners at the same time.

Another example of momentum is during a point, say you chip and charge on a short second serve and as your moving in the first shot comes back to you at the net and you hit it crosscourt and continue to move in closer to the net going past your partner, if the next ball starts to go to your partner's side of the court—crossover and take it. You're the one who has the momentum of moving in and you are now closer to the ball then your partner, so you can direct the traffic and go for it. Cross the middle and hit the next shot and if you don't put it away remember you still have the momentum so try to get the next ball also. Keep moving forward or in the direction of the ball until you put it away. Your partner won't mind that you crossed in front of them if you end the point.

The 'I' Formation

I started teaching the 'I' formation tactical play back in 1992 to my doubles teams that weren't playing true attacking style doubles but were still looking for other aggressive ways to end points quickly. The 'I' formation is a play that can do just that, end a point quickly, if you and your partner are playing in the one up one back formation and if you are communicating well as a team.

To execute this play during a point, from a one up/ one back formation, the back partner must hit a shot that allows the net partner to get positioned directly on the middle line of the frontcourt. The back partner then must get positioned directly behind the net partner at the baseline. This formation is called the 'I' and with the ball in the opponents backcourt the net partner now tries to take the next shot no matter to which side of the middle it is hit to and the back partner then switches to the opposite side of the net partner to balance out the court in case the net partner does not put the ball away. The trick is hitting the right shot to put your team into the 'I' formation. It has to be a deep shot to the backcourt to allow time to set up the formation.

Top Five Plays to get into the 'I' formation

Return the serve with a lob over the net players head. This is the easiest and fastest way to get into the 'I' formation.

During a crosscourt rally with both teams in a one up/one back formation, send a lob over the net players head.

Hit a high topspin shot crosscourt that bounces high over the baseline.

If the opposing team is playing both back hit a deep topspin down the middle of the backcourt that has plenty of airtime either in it's flight or bounce.

If the opposing team is playing both players up then hit a lob over either player.

As you can see, the lob is the best shot to use to set up your team in the 'I' formation. The reason is because the ball goes in high to the backcourt in an arch that the opponents must track and can't watch what you are doing on your side of the net. Once your team is in position there are two rules you must follow: one, the partner at the net must be ready to pounce

on any shot the opponent hits and two, the backcourt partner must be ready to cover any shot the net partner can't reach. If you both are committed to these two rules then you and your partner will be able to end points quicker and aggressively by using the 'I' formation.

Coach's Notebook:

Early Ages (5-9)—If there are sufficient layers to the five fundamentals then by all means start practicing shot combinations, working on patterns and begin developing tactical plays to use when serving and receiving. Why serving and receiving situations first? Because these are two areas in your game where you will need to develop weapons and it's two areas that every young player struggles with when starting tournament competition. Learning tactical plays either on the serve or return can be developed well before your junior player plays his or her first tournament which can decrease the double faulting and missed returns that plague a lot of young players. Practice baseline shot combinations and winning shots from the strokes and shots that are in advanced stages of development. A good drill to get in the habit of doing at this stage is to play practice service games by yourself until you can win a set without double faulting.

Jr Tournament Level Player—Every match played offers you the chance to play a different style of player, which means using different tactical plays to win points. My advice here is to put on as many layers of match play as possible. If you lose in the first round of the main draw then go play the back draw, if there is one offered, to get more matches.
Player Note: I like to see junior level tournament players play between 60-80 competitive matches per year. The importance is that you get the experience of trying the different tactics and strategies that you are using in your practices. Your game plan is in the development stage so be prepared to make changes in your game plan if you are having trouble beating certain types of players.

I was working with a player who had a terrible flaw in her fore-hand stroke. As I began to change it one day in practice, she stopped and said to me, "But coach, that's how I've hit it all my life." Let me tell you I had a pretty good laugh on the inside that day from her statement because that little girl was only eleven years old. Her entire tennis life consisted of about four years of layers.

Moral of the story: In order to improve, you really have to be open to change at this early stage of your tennis career especially if you are not winning. Know this; Pete Sampras changed from a two handed backhand to a one handed backhand at the age of 13 and Venus Williams changed her entire forehand grip and stroke one month before a Grand Slam.

As far as doubles goes you should be playing doubles at every tournament to hone in on your volleying skills as well as getting extra serving and returning practice. At this point in your game you need the most playing experience layers you can get. Keep in mind, a lot of great players got their first ever Grand Slam titles in doubles.

Pro Player Beginnings—You should have your top five shot combinations for your forehand side and backhand side and your top five ways you like to win points off your serve and off your return down at this point in your career. But that doesn't mean you can relax on those winning ways. Add defensive patterns and offensive attacks to your game plan. Remember this game changes every six months or so as new players with different playing styles are constantly coming into the game. Keep working on adding new tactical plays to your already long list and work harder at strategizing to beat players who have given you trouble in the past.

In the beginning of your Pro career you should play doubles at every tournament you enter. Why? For one, you need the extra practice of hitting your serves and returns against different types of players. Two, at some tournaments practice court time is unavailable and playing doubles will get you extra court time. Three, you'll make some good friends that you can practice with, travel with and socialize with, as the tour can sometimes be a lonely place.

CHAPTER TEN

Winning Ways

Once your ball striking and shot making skills are polished and your movement is near perfect then it's up to your layers of focused practices and winning experiences to get you through the tough matches. Your match play performance now becomes the measuring tool that you and everyone else will use to measure your success. All your off court training and on court hard work that you've put into your game both physically and mentally must come out in each opportunity you have to perform. And that's exactly what each match should be to you now as an accomplished player, an opportunity to show off all your acquired athletic, mental and overall tennis skills through your performance. All your goals and how you have planned to reach those goals is also on the line each and every time you step onto the court to perform and that brings in the last major road block that you and every other athlete on game day must learn to overcome, pressure.

No player can step onto the court or into a game and say that they don't feel some amount of pressure. It's a natural reaction that every player of every sport has when they are put on the spot to perform, to show if they have been truly working hard in their practices or whether they have been just going through the motions. The player who has just been going through the motions will undoubtedly feel more pressure because that player's inner self will be full of doubt at knowing that he or she hasn't properly prepared. That player will only have the hope that his or her best performance will come out during the match and hope is just not good enough in the New Game.

That great performance that you want to have needs to come from an inner self confidence that you have inside you to do exactly what you are capable of doing. A confidence that starts on the practice court where you have disciplined your game in order to stay focused on the goal that now lies before you, winning the match. That type of intense focus must become an unconsciously competent state of being on the practice court so that on game day when its time for you to perform; you can focus on the particulars of the match itself like, your opponent, the ball, the surface and the weather conditions and not have to hope that your best performance shines through.

No player, however, can stay completely focused, motivated and confident throughout his or her entire career. There are going to be times when the pressure from some source of the tennis world or life gets in the way and causes your performance to fade. If the pressure persists then you may even fall into the dreaded *slump* and lose confidence in yourself or in your game.

If that happens it's important that you be honest with yourself in order to properly diagnose the problem. You have to ask yourself the tough questions like: Have you been putting enough effort into your on-court or off-court training? Have you lost your self-discipline or determination? Are you putting too much pressure on yourself to perform above your abilities? Once you find where your problem lies then you can take the necessary steps to get yourself out of your slump and then do this: write it down. Write down what you went through and what it was that got you out of that dreaded slump. Maybe it was something positive your coach said or a new practice routine or maybe it was getting yourself in better shape by training harder off the court or adding new drills to your on-court practices. Whatever it was, writing it down will aid you later on if something like that happens again. We've all been there so know this; you will eventually return to your winning ways whether or not you can hang in there mentally to ride out the slump is the real question.

Vincent Spadea

Vince Spadea is considered a journeyman on the men's ATP tour. His thirteen year career has been full of many ups and downs as he has been in and out of the top fifty several times in his career and suffered a few slumps. Although Vince doesn't own any Grand Slam titles in his 223 events played, he does own a record on the men's tour that he would probably rather not. He has the record for the most main draw first round losses in a row.

Now there are a lot of players who would have thought that their careers were coming to an end after setting a record like that and maybe Vince thought this a little bit too at times, I don't know. What I do know however is that he is still grinding away on the men's tour chasing his ultimate goal and dream and at the beginning of 2004 he came one step closer. Playing in the Franklin Templeton Tennis Classic tournament he beat the number one player in the world, Andy Roddick, and three other top twenty players on his way to the tournament finals where he claimed his first ever men's tour singles title.

A great lesson for all of us in determination and perseverance. Way to go Vince!

Over the years I have documented those up and down experiences that my players have gone through in their quests to becoming the perfect tennis players and in the pursuit of their ultimate goals and dreams. From the winning streaks when confidence was high and nothing could go wrong to the slumps when confidence was low and nothing could go right. From those experiences, I have come up with the following winning ways and recipes.

On Dreams and Goals

• Dream that you can—Before you can achieve anything you have to Dream it first! If your dream is to win the US Open, then see yourself holding up the US Open trophy high over your head while a stadium packed crowd gives you a standing ovation for your great performance. Then once you've dreamed it, you can set short and long term goals and make the proper plans to achieving it.

• Put your long term dream goals and short term goals down on paper—By doing this you have a written contract with yourself to do what ever it takes to achieve those goals. Don't forget to sign and date it.

• Once you achieve a goal check it off—When a goal is achieved check it off your list and replace it with another goal that is on your path towards your ultimate dream goal. If your goal is to add ten pounds of muscle mass and you do it, then give yourself an award for your achievement and then move on to the next goal or try to improve upon that goal which you just achieved.

• Don't set goals you can't achieve—If your list of goals doesn't have any checks on it after one year then maybe you set goals that are unrealistic of your ability. Reassess your goals and make sure you have some goals that you can achieve in: 3 months, 8 months, 12 months, 1 ½ years and 3 years.

• Find out what drives you towards your Dreams—People that accomplish great things are driven. They have a fire within them that keeps them focused on their goals and dreams. What is it that drives you? Remember that your goals and dreams are just that your goals and dreams. To be truly driven you must achieve for yourself and not for anyone else's expectations of you. Achieving to please others is a fire that is easily extinguished.

• Discipline yourself—You won't accomplish many of your goals or get far down the path of your dream if you don't have self-discipline. Being able to say no to that candy bar and yes to ten more crunches is key ingredient to dream achieving.

On Focus

There are many factors that determine what may happen during a point, a game or a set but the fact still remains that in tennis nothing is for certain and because of that fact a player must stay focused on his or her opponent as well as the ball at all times. My I.P.D.E. recipe is one way to do just that, stay focused.

The I.P.D.E. Recipe

IDENTIFY BY WATCHING OPONENT

I= IDENTIFY

This is the first and most important part of the recipe because before you have the opportunity to strike the ball your opponent has to hit it over the net and inside the lines first. While this is taking place your ability to identify three factors will greatly improve your response to their shot.

The first factor and easiest to identify is spin. While focusing on your opponent's racquet you should be able to see whether the ball is above or below the racquet head right before contact. Above the racquet head means that a topspin stroke is being hit and if below the racquet head then an under spin is being hit. As we've learned earlier in this book, a topspin stroke bounces high and forward where as an under spin stroke bounces much lower and skids. Because you have properly identified the balls spin you can now identify the other two factors.

The second factor you must identify is direction. While an opponent's body position will give away some of the direction you must also look at which side of the ball the racquet head is on and how far out in front of the body is the contact point. If the racquet head is on the inside of the ball and just slightly in front of the body then you can expect a down the line or inside out type shot but if the racquet head is on the outside of the ball and farther out from the body the you should look for a crosscourt type shot. Lastly watch the shoulders for an early or late opening to the net. An

early opening can often mean a crosscourt type shot and a late opening is often used for down the line or straightforward type shots. Now that you have identified the spin and direction of your opponents shot you can now identify the last factor.

The last factor to identify is speed. This can be identified by the racquet speed distance through the ball. If the follow through is cut short in any way the ball will have less speed then a follow through that extends fully towards its target. You have now identified your opponent's shot and can begin the next part of the recipe.

P= PREDICT

Once you have identified the shot you can now predict how that shot will affect you on your side of the net. If you now know the balls spin, direction and speed then you can predict how it will bounce, where it is going in relation to your position and whether or not it's fast enough or deep enough to force you into a defensive or neutralizing situation or slow enough or short enough to allow you to be on the offensive. Your entire preparation, court position and footwork to the ball rely on whether or not you have identified and predicted every factor accurately. If you have identified and predicted accurately, then you can begin the next part of the recipe.

GETTING READY

D= DETERMINE

If you have identified and predicted properly then you can now search your arsenal of strokes and shots that you own and determine which one will counter your opponents shot best according to two factors: where your opponent is positioned and where you have determined your next shot should be hit. A poor decision of shot or placement will have you on the defensive, cause an error or result in a missed opportunity. Once you have determined your shot and where to hit it then you can act out and complete the recipe.

**PREPARING TO HIT THE
DETERMINED SHOT**

E=EXECUTE

This, of course, is what separates the great players from the average players; the ability to execute the determined shot on command. Once you have determined the best shot to use you must be able to then execute it. And that is why a player must practice over and over again the same shots and shot combinations so that when it happens in a match it is as comfortable as an old pair of shoes even in the most pressure filled situations. Even the simplest of shots can become very difficult to execute if there is the added pressure of say a U S Open trophy on the line. Let's look at a couple of examples of players who completed the recipe.

Venus Williams was playing Irina Spirlea in the semifinals of the 1997 U S Open. It was the tiebreaker of the third and final set. Spirlea got a ball that she felt comfortable with and so she hit an offensive under spin short crosscourt backhand for what looked like a winner, but Venus had identified the spin, the direction and the speed of the shot and she knew she could run it down. She predicted the angle and that low bounce of the shot would not allow her to recover since she would be running at full speed just to get to it. While running to it she then determined that her best response knowing there was no recovery was to blast a topspin backhand down the line for a winner. If she missed the match was over and Spirlea was on to the finals. She didn't miss however and executed the shot perfectly. She ended up winning the match completing the formula as a true champion would.

EXECUTING THE SHOT

In another example, Jimmy Connors was playing Paul Haarhuis in the quarterfinals of the 1991 U S Open. Harrhuis hit a great approach shot to the Connors forehand. Connors identified how well Harrhuis had hit the shot and predicting its depth he determined the best shot would be a defensive lob. He executed the shot perfectly so that Harrhuis could not put the ball away and Connors was able to stay in the point and eventually win the point. It was a turning point and momentum builder for Connors who went on to win the match.

Both examples start with the number one element in the I.P.D.E. recipe, Identify. Once you have hit the ball to your desired shot location your job has just begun, don't go to sleep mentally. You can gain so much knowledge about your opponent if you focus on their every move. Watch their shoulder turn, their knee bend, the position of their racquet in the backswing, the speed of their swing, the angle at which they made contact with the ball, their stance and finally their entire body language. You need to be able to watch all this and then determine your next move all within a split second. The great ones do it because they practice doing it each and every day. You can't say to yourself one day, "ok today I think I'm going to focus more on my opponent's execution of his or her shot." No that just won't do it as focus needs to be an every time occurrence, a daily habit a way of life.

In searching for new ways to increase focus in my players over the years I have tried some interestingly fun, cutting-edge different and oddly strange experiments trying to enhance ball-striking performance. Leaving out the oddly strange, here are my top five, of what I now call, alternative focus drills.

Top Five Alternative Focus Drills

In Your Head—A player rallies from the baseline wearing headphones and listening to motivational music and inspirational quotes. (Mental awareness enhancer)

One Eyed Shots—A player hits volleys, groundstrokes and overheads with one eye covered by an eye patch. Hit each shot or stroke for ten minutes and then hit without the eye patch. (Vision focus enhancer)

Night Light—At night, using only a blinking strobe light to light the court, a player hits a variety of shots for 20 minutes. Then turn on normal lighting and hit for 20 minutes. (repeat)(Visual focus enhancer)

White vs Yellow—Using only white balls, a player practices all shots for 20 minutes. Then switch to yellow balls and practice 20 minutes. (repeat)
XX OO—Mark a big X or O on a bunch of balls and add them to your practice basket. As you are rallying from the baseline try to pick out the Xs and Os during the drill until all have been found. (Visual focus enhancer)

ON Game Day

The great champions of all sports have a common bond; they all know how to bring out their best performance on game day. Bringing out your best performance on game day is what matters most to the accomplished player. A week's worth of bad practices won't matter much if on game day you are performing at your best. All pro players know that a poor performance on game day means a smaller paycheck and an early plane ticket home, so when a good performance happens you better believe me they remember exactly what they did before stepping onto the court that day. Some players develop wacky rituals and superstitions from great performance days while others try not to get too superstitious and simply try and stick to a more relaxed but consistent routine. A routine that begins well before stepping onto the court. Junior players take note; you need a routine that has you breaking a sweat and completely warmed up before you even step onto the court to start the match warm up. If that means hitting for an hour with your coach or doing sprints and jump roping in the parking lot of the tournament site, then do it. You need to be on the attack from the moment the first ball is struck. The pro players know this and never count on the match warm up to be enough to get them ready for a great performance. Take a look at this typical game day routine you might go through, if you were a pro player playing at the US Open in New York City.
• *6:30am* hotel wake up call.
• *7:00am* you throw on sweats and a hat and go down to breakfast at the hotel restaurant. You meet with your coach there to go over every detail of the day: first practice, transportation, lunch, pre-match stretch routines, second warm-up, match attire, press conferences, match time, post match stretch and rub down, dinner and any other detail that could happen on this day. (It's important to have every detail considered and planned so that you can focus on your game plan of your upcoming opponent.)

• *7:45am* you catch a ride with player transportation from the city to Flushing Meadows. With a tennis bag full of clothes and accessories for a day of activity on your back and headphones on your head you go to the players locker room to drop off your gear. (3 shirts, 3 shorts, extra socks, wristbands, sweatshirt, book, cd player, power bar and everything and anything else.)

• *9:00am-* your first warm-up is approximately a one hour hit with your coach or practice partner. A typical session: 5 minutes of short court, 5 minutes of crosscourt backhands, 5 minutes of crosscourt forehands, 5 minutes of down the line forehands, 5 minutes of down the line backhands, 10 minutes of serves, 10 minutes of returns, 10 minutes of volleys & overheads and 10 minutes of point play.

• *10:00am* –your first shower of the day, a nutrition bar and a change into relaxing clothes to wait until match time which is 2nd on court 5 after

• *11am.* So really you must be ready to go by 11:00 in case a player in the first match gets injured in the first game or two and has to default. That would mean you are on court at 11:30am and that's why you should eat a little something incase lunch is optioned out. If the first match goes the usual 2 hours then you won't be on until 1pm and can have a nice lunch while you wait.

• *12:30pm-* you've had lunch and see that the match on your court looks to be going the distance, so you head out to practice court 1 and get in a light hit with another player who also plays 2nd on as you do. This is not your opponent, as you don't warm up with your opponent ever. This warm up is optional and shouldn't be more then 30 minutes of light hitting and serving.

• *1:00pm-* you head to the locker room and take shower number two, if needed to refresh you, as the first match on your court is at 5-5 in the third. You have one of the tournament trainers stretch you out and then you find a quiet spot to focus on your game plan of the upcoming match that you and your coach have already gone over.

• *1:20-* your match is called and you are escorted through the crowd outside the player building by a tournament official. You get your first glimpse of your opponent who joins you in your walk to the court escorted by her own official. She is a seeded player who you've met before. She is a great player and a nice person you think to yourself but today she is the enemy. A player who is trying to take something that you have deemed is yours, the tournament title.

• *1:30-* you are on the court and now warming up for the third time. By this time you are loose and ready to go and this warm up is more about burning off some nerves and anxiety of the situation. You work up a quick sweat and the umpire calls, "Time."

• *3:55-* your match is over. You ended up pulling off the upset 7-6 in the third and have gone through all the shirts in your bag. You head to the showers and have a post match stretch with a trainer.

• *4:45-* you are finally starting to come down from the high of your great performance when an official grabs you for your required post match press conference.

• *5:15-* you catch a ride back to your hotel in the city with a bag full of dirty laundry and an empty spot in your stomach. Luckily you didn't sign up for doubles or else you would probably just be going back on the court back at the tennis complex.

• *6:45-* you arrive back at your hotel where you are scheduled to meet some friends for dinner. You have just enough time to change and meet them in the lobby by 7pm.

• *7:30pm* you have dinner, which is essential to refueling your body for tomorrow's match, which is scheduled for 3rd on after 11am.

• *9:00pm* you're back at your hotel room where you watch some TV for about an hour before calling it a day. Because you're 3rd on tomorrow you get a wake up call for 7:30am.

• *10pm* – You're done for the day only to wake up tomorrow and do it all over again.

On Big Tournaments -7 Rounds to Glory

Many players have learned how to perform well enough on game days to win small tournaments or even a match or two within a big tournament, but to win a big tournament, like a Supernational, WTA Tier one event, Jr Grand Slam, ATP Masters event or a Grand Slam tournament, it takes careful planning

and incredible mental strength. It takes your best performance steadily maintained and layered upon through seven grueling and increasingly difficult rounds over the course of ten days to two weeks.

To get through each difficult round you'll need to put yourself in what I like to call *The Performance Zone*! You know that zone where there is no fear of anyone and no second-guessing of your own game, only self-confidence and intense focus. That zone where all you see is your opponent, the ball and the lines and nothing else. That's the zone you'll need to layer upon as you go through each round.

My players all know about the big tournaments and the seven grueling rounds it takes to become a part of tennis history, because when it comes to our most difficult on court and off court drills, we always complete seven rounds. And each round gets increasingly more difficult to remind them that so will each round of any big tournament. They know to plan on more difficult matches as they go through the big tournaments so that they won't get caught hoping, each round, for a good performance to shine through. They also know to always keep in mind that what worked against yesterday's opponent might not win a game or set against today's opponent.

Player Note: Big tournaments are the true test to your overall game and your practices should be planned throughout the year so that you are performing at your best for each event.

The biggest tournaments in tennis are known as the Grand Slams, which are: The Australian Open, The French Open, Wimbledon and The US Open. Win one of these and people will remember you, more importantly, win one of these tournaments and you've achieved one of the highest of goals in the sport of tennis. Remember, that ultimate goal of winning a Grand Slam that you've had since before you played your first junior tournament? It's what started you on this path to the pros in the first place; so when you find yourself playing in one, don't be afraid to achieve it. That Grand Slam dream goal should be scribbled down somewhere on a goal sheet or in your junior tournament journal. Don't have one? Here's a copy of the one I have my players fill out.

GOAL SHEET

Write down your top five goals for each time period listed at the top of the
sheet. This can be a mix of personal goals such as, body strength, shot making and footwork or speed goals as well as tournaments you'd like to win
or a ranking you'd like to achieve or even a player or players you'd like to
beat. Then, on the bottom half of the sheet list your ultimate goals for the
next 3 yr, 5 yr and lifetime periods.

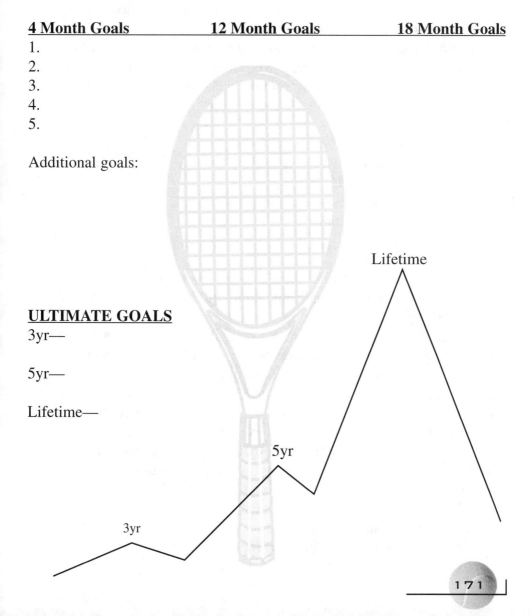

4 Month Goals	**12 Month Goals**	**18 Month Goals**
1.		
2.		
3.		
4.		
5.		

Additional goals:

Lifetime

ULTIMATE GOALS

3yr—

5yr—

Lifetime—

5yr

3yr

On Mental Toughness

Always expect to win—The great players always expect to win every time they step onto the court. They have a belief within them that they are more talented, more disciplined, better prepared and in better physical condition than anyone else in the tournament. Because they believe that, they go into each match with a mental edge and if they do happen to lose believe me they are shocked.

My hometown university used to have a motivational motto for their basketball program called M.T.X.E., which meant: mental, toughness, xtra, effort. I changed that old motto slightly into a recipe that I now like to use for the players in my program who show an exceptional performance in their practices and matches by coming back when behind or by chasing down that extra ball in drills. My motto reads:

The M.T. Double E. Recipe
  M=Mental
  T=Toughness
  E=Exceptional
  E=Effort

One of the great things about the sport of tennis is there is no time clock. You can't run out of time while you're playing a match. For that reason you should never ever give up trying, even if your opponent is taking it to you and you find yourself down a set and a break in the match. If you keep hustling to get every ball and keep trying different tactical plays you may outlast your opponent's fitness level or mental level or find something tactically that begins to work. There have been some great comebacks over the years by players who had the mental toughness to comeback from what looked like sure defeat. Those players exemplified the M.T.E.E. recipe. For example: On the men's ATP tour, Jimmy Connors was down 6-1,6-1,4-1 to Michael Pernfors one year at Wimbledon before he found the right tactical game plan and put forth an exceptional effort to comeback and win the match in the fifth set. On the women's WTA tour, Mary Joe Fernandez came back once from 6-0,5-0 down to Gabriella Sabatini at the French Open to win in the final set. Both examples are about as close as you can come to losing before turning things around. It takes incredible mental toughness not to throw in the towel and say that it's just not your day when you are getting beaten that badly, but if you show a little M.T.E.E. and hang in there you never know what may happen. And even if you only win a few more games you may learn something very important or useful about your-self or your opponent that will lead you to victory the next time. The worst thing you can do is give in to defeat. It doesn't help your inner you nor does it add any experience layers to your game and besides, nobody likes a quitter.

On Pressure
• Pressure is a part of every athlete's life, so embrace it, and make it yours.
• If you can control it you will thrive on it and you will succeed.
• Never use the pressure from others as an excuse for losing. The only rea-son there is any outside pressure is because you have a chance to do some-thing big. Remember that others expectations of you are not why you're playing anyway.
• Realize pressure situations and learn to love them. You want to have the attitude that the more pressure there is the better you will play.
• Pressure from within usually comes about when you know you haven't properly prepared for the performance at hand.
• Practice playing under pressure.
• Don't pretend there is no pressure. Break points, game points and set points are all full of pressure and denying it won't help you to play better.
• To relieve pressure, don't be so concerned with winning or losing. Be more concerned with your performance. If it is good then you will win.
• Remember your opponent feels pressure during big point situations also.

A Life Formula
So, do you still want to be a tennis pro? As you have read so far, it is no easy path. If it were, then everyone would do it. You've now learned a lot of what it takes to compete in the New Game and hopefully you have a more defined path in which to follow. But even when all is learned that can be learned there is still one formula that must be apparent in your plans if you are ever going to stand a chance at being successful in this sport or anything else in your life. That formula is:

Belief in yourself (x) Disciplined hard Work (+) Opportunities = Success

The first ingredient of the formula, Belief in yourself, is without a doubt the most important. Without it, you have no chance of being successful. The one thing that all successful people (Champions) have is a deep belief that they can achieve (win) no matter what the odds. They feel that there is nothing that they can't accomplish. They go into a match, a race, a business deal or a game, expecting to out perform their opponents each and every time and never doubt their offensive plays or their defensive strategies. They believe inside that their talent, in the end, is far greater then that of their opponents. Having that inner confidence is a key ingredient that separates the pretenders from the true contenders. Opponents and spectators will know by your performance how confident you are on the inside. They'll begin to refer to you as a competitor, a fighter, a someone with tremendous desire and hopefully they will eventually refer to you as a champion.

Belief will start you on your climb to the top of the mountain but it will take the discipline to work hard every day, ingredient number two, to fuel you there. I've seen many talented players reach the fullness of their talent and then fall by the wayside because they weren't willing to work hard everyday to improve upon what tennis talents they were given. If you're reading this and coasting along on just your talent then I can tell you right now you should not expect to ever win the Australian Open, Wimbledon, French Open or US Open titles. Those tournaments are won by tennis athletes who have not only disciplined their tennis games but also their entire lives. That ingredient of self-discipline is something that everyone has come across in their lives at some point, whether or not they were able or willing to practice it is another story.

The Righty and the Lefty

This is the story of two twin brothers, both tennis players, one a righty and the other a lefty.

Since the age of three both brothers showed a special interest in playing tennis ball games. Their parents seeing that interest, signed them up for their first lessons at the local tennis center where they both took similar group and private lessons from ages 5yrs to 10 yrs old. Although each of them developed tournament level games, it is clear to the locals that the lefty has more talent then the righty.

In the 12's junior division the lefty reaches a top ten national ranking where the righty ends the year ranked just inside the top 100. Both players feel enough success in the 12's and so they move up to the 14's division the following year.

The righty believes in himself and doesn't think his ranking reflects his true potential so he makes a personal decision to train harder and improve his weaknesses while adding to his strengths. He doubles his on court practice time hitting over a thousand balls a session and also adds an off court fitness program into his schedule.

The lefty goes about his normal casual practice schedule only putting the minimal effort into his game relying on his talent to again get him a national ranking. He too believes in his ability and has a strong confidence growing within. At the end of the year the lefty finishes inside the top twenty in the nation and the righty finishes inside the top fifty.

Now you may have thought that the lefty would have finished higher then his brother because he wasn't practicing as hard. But what you have to remember is that the lefty has the more talent and still believes he is the better player. The gap between the two brothers has closed however and the righty is developing the important ingredient of self-discipline as well as putting an increasing amount of valuable layers of hard practice time on his game.

The two brothers again move up a division and are both having good success. Half way through the year the righty re-evaluates his goals and decides to move up into the 18's division to get even tougher competition. He knows he will have to work twice as hard but is willing too in

order to advance his game to a higher level. The lefty decides to stay in the 16's division where he is having success by putting out only minimal effort.

The following year the two brothers both play in the 18's division. The righty has good success and by the halfway point is ranked in the top ten in the nation. The lefty struggles to crack the top one hundred and finds that he now can't beat the top players with his current game. He wants to go higher but doesn't have the self-discipline to put out the extra effort in retooling his game.

The righty who has developed good self-discipline and made goal setting a priority, pushes himself even harder to peak his game for the Junior Orange Bowl 18's, which he wins. The lefty loses early in the same tournament and then loses the desire and interest in his game and decides to call it quits so that he can pursue one of his other interests.

The story of the righty and lefty shows that if you have the self-discipline to work hard then you can take your talent a lot further then someone who has no self-discipline with exceptional talent. There are numerous stories throughout history of talented people like the lefty, who did not succeed because: a) they didn't set goals and make plans to achieve, b) they didn't have self-discipline c) they didn't work hard enough or weren't persistent enough, to see their dream come true.

Follow Your Path to the Pros

There are many different paths you can take to reach your dream of playing professional tennis. To help a player in his or her competitive development layers there is a tournament structure that ranges from the junior level circuit to the pro level. In the United States it's the USTA that is the governing body that runs the junior circuit of tournaments that offers events in the following age groups in both boys & girls divisions – 10's, 12's, 14's, 16's, 18's. The USTA also runs lower tiered satellite pro events and the fourth Grand Slam, the US Open.

A standard way of thinking is that a player should play in his or her age group until old enough to move up into the next division. I believe differently and feel a player should move up as soon as outstanding perform-ances within a division necessitate the move. But when to move up is still a big question and decision for most parents, coaches and junior players and you have to evaluate what your goals really are as a player to answer that question correctly. Do you want to win all the 12's nationals and super nationals before moving on? Do you want to travel internationally and try to have major success playing junior events that are governed by the ITF to get a world junior ranking? Do you want to have a successful junior career and then move on to play in college? In answering these questions you have to go back to that goal sheet you filled out and read again what ultimate goal is written down.

If your ultimate goal is to play pro-level tennis then the answer to all the above questions should be, no. No you do not want to win all the 12's nationals and supernationals because if you win just one then you should move up and start playing 14's or 16's. A better goal would be to win one big 12's event and then move up. No you do not want to have a successful junior career and then move on to play college because if you have a successful junior career then pro circuit tournament opportunities will present themselves and you wouldn't want to miss your window to the pro ranks. Finally, no you don't want to travel internationally trying to win every ITF junior tournament because if your junior ranking moves up inter-nationally that will only help you in the ITF tournament system and you'll miss opportunities in the USA. It may sound as if I'm against the whole junior tournament system, but I'm not. I do believe that you need a balance of competitive junior play as long as it fits into your plans and goals. What I am against is seeing good players get ruined in the junior system because they fall into what I call the junior tennis traps.

The Junior tennis traps are: 1.rivalries within your own age group, 2.being grouped together with other players in your division, not standing out and getting lost in your division, 3. Putting other junior play-ers on a pedestal, 4.overachieving within a certain age division 5. Loss of desire/burning out.

These traps can bound a player to a career that begins and ends at the junior level, if not avoided. You mustn't get caught up in all the hype of a high junior ranking or trying to win every junior event if in fact your goal is to play at the pro-level. I believe you need to balance your early jun-

ior playing experience with your development layers and then get out of junior tennis as soon as you can and get on with what you set out to do in the first place. Some players will need more junior-level experience then others and you know what, that's fine. Like I said before, every player has his or her own special needs and circumstances to deal with, so if you need more junior experience then get more but just remember this; once you are on the pro tour, your experience layers start all over again. That's right, the pro players play differently and are much more disciplined. That's why I like a player to start playing pro-level tournaments as soon as they're of age, even if their development layers aren't ready, so they can experience for themselves what it's like to be out there and to see who is out there. Even if they don't get out of the qualifying draws in the beginning, at least they are seeing how the main draw players are practicing and preparing before, during and after the event. That experience will help the player make the leap completely out of juniors much less of a shock when the time is right.

So now, all you have to do, is figure out which path is right for you to follow to achieve your ultimate goal. Remember to consider your own special needs and circumstances, which must be evaluated and considered in both the physical and mental aspects of your game when choosing your path. Then, set realistic goals, make the proper plans to get you there and finally work hard. How you are going to achieve your goals is what makes up your plans and practice sessions and proper plans and practice are the strings that tie everything together towards your ultimate goal. In other words, don't try and wing it. That's why you're reading this book, right? **Player Note**: When making up plans and practice sessions, be sure to surround yourself with coaches and people who not only support your goals but who also are after you, achieving your dreams. A good support group around you will make the journey much more enjoyable.

On Practice

Speaking of practice sessions, remember what you read in chapter one, there are no shortcuts. Practice sessions are the key ingredients to putting developing layers on your overall tennis skills. For those players who are already playing high-level junior to pro-level tournaments, here are five sample days of practice, for an off-week, which means there is no upcoming tournament.

Day 1

Futuremetrics 6:30am

1:00-4:15 on-court practice

Stretch and warm up by running the lines of two courts—player starts on one line and, without stepping off the lines, must run up, down and across until all the court's lines have been touched. Then on to the next court and so on until four half court sections have been run.

Serves—Player alone for 15 minutes of private serving

1:30-Warm up hitting:

Short court hitting to warm up topspin wrist snaps and get in the hitting mood.

Baseline hitting up the middle.

Crosscourt forehands

Crosscourt backhands

Down the line backhands

Down the line forehands

Combination Hitting:

Forehand combo with a crosscourt base and a down the line finish

Backhand combo with a crosscourt base and a down the line finish

Patterns:

Crosscourt down the line drill

2:30-Daily shot emphasis:

Work on the mechanics of a particular shot or stroke that you don't own.

Work on incorporating that shot or stroke into a combination or pattern.

3:00—Serves and Returns:

Practice all three serve mechanics

Increase power on all serves

Practice placement of all three serves

Return forehands and backhands from the deuce court

Return forehands and backhands from the add court

Point Play and Situations:

Player serves to deuce court and plays point

Player serves to add court and plays point

Player returns from deuce court and plays point

Player returns form add court and plays point

Player returns from a 30-30 situation and plays out game

Player serves from a 30-30 situation and plays out game
4:00—(On-court Conditioning☹Optional)
7 rounds of footwork
Stretch and cool down

Day 2

Futuremetrics 6:30am
1:00-4:15 on-court practice
Stretch and warm up by running the lines of two courts—player starts on one line and, without stepping off the lines, must run up, down and across until all the court's lines have been touched. Then on to the next court and so on until four half court sections have been run.
Serves—Player alone for 15 minutes of private serving
1:30-Warm up hitting:
Short court hitting to warm up topspin wrist snaps and get in the hitting mood.
Baseline hitting up the middle.
Crosscourt forehands
Crosscourt backhands
Down the line backhands
Down the line forehands
Combination Hitting:
Forehand inside-out combinations
Backhand inside-out combinations
2:20 Serves and Returns:
Practice all three serve mechanics
Increase power on all serves
Practice placement of all three serves
Return forehands and backhands from the deuce court
Return forehands and backhands from the add court
3:00 Patterns:
2-10 shots crosscourt then one down the line then repeat off a crosscourt response.
Daily shot emphasis:
Volleys
Overheads

Point Play and Situations:
Player serves to add court and plays point
Player returns from add court and plays point
Player serves at 40-30 and plays out game
Player returns at 30-40 and plays out game
4:00—(On-court Conditioning☹Optional)
7 rounds of footwork
Stretch and cool down

Day 3

Futuremetrics 6:30am
1:00-4:15 on-court practice
Stretch and warm up by running the lines of two courts—player starts on one line and, without stepping off the lines, must run up, down and across until all the court's lines have been touched. Then on to the next court and so on until four half court sections have been run.
Serves—Player alone for 15 minutes of private serving
1:30-Warm up hitting:
Short court hitting to warm up topspin wrist snaps and get in the hitting mood.
Baseline hitting up the middle.
Crosscourt forehands
Crosscourt backhands
Down the line backhands
Down the line forehands
2:00 Serves and Returns:
Practice all three serve mechanics
Increase power on all serves
Practice placement of all three serves
Return forehands and backhands from the deuce court
Return forehands and backhands from the add court
Combination Hitting:
Forehand down the line combinations
Backhand down the line combinations
3:00 Patterns:
Player is only allowed to play neutralizing and defensive shots (no win-

ners) while a coach or practice partner tries to play all offensive type shots. Then switch shots.

Point Play and Situations:

Player serves to deuce court and plays point

Player returns from add court and plays point

Player serves at 0-30 and plays out game

Player returns at 30-0 and plays out game

4:00   (On-court Conditioning☺Optional)

7 rounds of footwork

Stretch and cool down

Day 4

Futuremetrics 6:30am

1:00-4:15 on-court practice

Stretch and warm up by running the lines of two courts—player starts on one line and, without stepping off the lines, must run up, down and across until all the court's lines have been touched. Then on to the next court and so on until four half court sections have been run.

Serves—Player alone for 15 minutes of private serving

1:30 Serves and Returns:

Practice all three serve mechanics

Increase power on all serves

Practice placement of all three serves

Return forehands and backhands from the deuce court

Return forehands and backhands from the add court

2:30 Hitting:

Baseline hitting up the middle.

Crosscourt forehands

Crosscourt backhands

Down the line backhands

Down the line forehands

Combination Hitting:

Forehand approach down the line/volley

Backhand approach down the line/volley

3:00 Shot emphasis:

Lunge & Kick returns with recovery

Rip and charge returns of second serves
Point Play and Situations:
Player returns second serves from deuce court and plays out point
Player returns second serves from add court and plays out point
Player returns at 30-30 with a second serve and plays out game
Player returns at 30-40 with a second serve and plays out game
4:00—(On-court Conditioning☹Optional)
7 rounds of footwork
Stretch and cool down

Day 5

Futuremetrics 6:30am
1:00-4:15 on-court practice
Stretch and warm up by running the lines of two courts—player starts on one line and, without stepping off the lines, must run up, down and across until all the court's lines have been touched. Then on to the next court and so on until four half court sections have been run.
Serves—Player alone for 15 minutes of private serving
1:30 Hitting:
Short court hitting
Baseline hitting up the middle.
Crosscourt forehands
Crosscourt backhands
Down the line backhands
Down the line forehands
Combination Hitting:
Drop shot then lob
Short angles then lob
Shot emphasis:
Lobs
Drop shots and short angles
2:45 Serves and Returns:
Practice all three serve mechanics
Increase power on all serves
Practice placement of all three serves
Return forehands and backhands from the deuce court

Return forehands and backhands from the add court
<u>Point Play and Situations:</u>
Player serves first serves only to deuce court and plays out point
Player serves first serves only to add court and plays out point
Player serves at 40-0 and plays out game(Play to 6 games)
Player returns at 0-40 and plays out game(play to 6 games)
<u>4:00—(On-court Conditioning☹Optional)</u>
7 rounds of footwork
Stretch and cool down

Player Note: The time at which serves and returns are hit during practice changes regularly so that you practice your serve at different conditioning and focus levels. All point play and situational play can be substituted with playing practice sets.

Final War Lessons

So as you have read, there's more to this game of tennis then just hitting the ball back and forth across the net. Today's game is an athletic battle and a mental war out there on the courts and as a player you must be prepared to go into the trenches daily with your best weapons and your most positive mental attitude if you expect to survive.

The following is a list of my favorite, of what I like to call, *war lessons on a player's life,* that I've learned over the last thirty-some years. I don't claim to be the creator of all of them as some are as old as athletics themselves, but I do claim that they can be used regularly for any sport you are participating in as well as in many areas of your life. May they help you to become the next great tennis player athlete of the New Game.

On A Player's Life

Hit balls everyday to add layers to your game, if to be a pro player is your goal. A 7-layer cake without the layers is a pancake.
Avoid those who do not understand or believe in your quest.

- Find a good coach. Inspiration, technique, success, strategy and desire rub off.
- When you're having a bad practice day, give yourself a break. Remember Rome wasn't built in a day.
- Do something positive everyday to advance your game, your character, your goals or your knowledge.
- Enjoy the development years of your game; that climb to the top of the tennis mountain. It's those years, that long second act, and not the big finish that makes a life.
- Set high goals for yourself and then attach deadlines to achieving each one.
- After a bad loss, remember, there's always tomorrow for dreams to come true.
- Don't make excuses, find solutions.
- Play more if you want more victories.
- Don't rush your game to the pro market. Make sure you are ready.
- Play for yourself. Not for your parents, not for your coaches, not for anyone else but you.
- Love the game not the money or the fame. Money can be earned a lot easier and those who have fame live their lives in the fear of losing it.
- Never celebrate a bad win.
- Maintain the long vision and don't be discouraged by the losses along the way.
- Accept responsibility for your failures. Learn from them and then move on. Don't make excuses or blame anyone or anything.
- Don't be quick to believe all those press releases about your talent. Desire and hard work may have had more to do with it.
- Never speak of your victories or achievements. If others speak fine, it will be heard tenfold.
- Beautiful strokes mean nothing if you haven't learned how to win with them.
- There is pleasure and pain in every situation. Be the optimist.
- Always play to win even in practice. Stop repeating losing patterns.
- Consistency in failure is no virtue.

• Do not put any player on a pedestal. It dwarfs you and gains you nothing.
• Run your own race. Stay focused on your goals not what others are doing.
• Never be satisfied in results that come up short of the goal. In every tournament there is only one winner.
• When you are out played give credit where credit is due.
• Dream that you can, then pursue that dream everyday with all your Heart.
• Never forget why you started playing tennis—-because it's Fun!

THE DRILL PAGES

The Drill:
The Georgia Star Footwork Drill

comment:

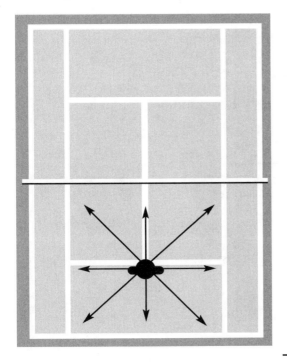

The Purpose:
Improves a player's quickness when moving within a 15 foot area. For building leg strength and endurance.

The Practice:
Player starts at the service line T in the middle of the court.
On the whistle the player has 43 seconds to complete the star.
Player sprints to each of the eight areas of the court and then back to the T after each area.
If on a clay court then the player should slide into each area and slide into the T.

The Drill:
Suicide Shuffles

comment:

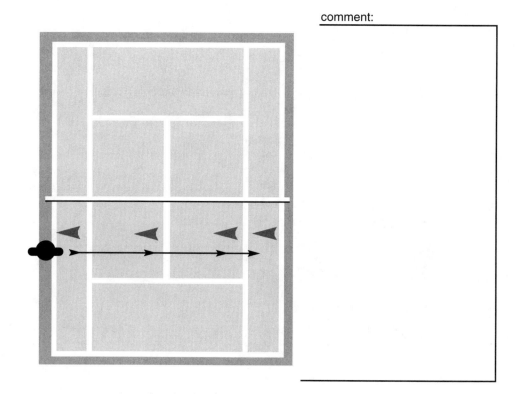

The Purpose:
Improves mobility in recovering and in moving laterally in areas of 15 feet or more.

The Practice:
Player starts on the doubles sideline.

Player shuffles and touches each line on the court returning each time to the doubles sideline.

Timed less than 25 seconds.

The Drill:

Two Ball Pick-Up

comment:

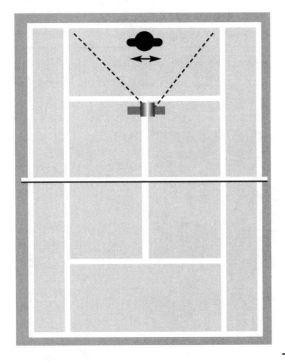

The Purpose:

Improves lateral movement and directional change. Works on the key fundamental of staying down.

The Practice

Coach or practice partner stands with two tennis balls at the service line area facing the player who is positioned at the baseline.

A ball is rolled to either side of the player.

The player shuffles laterally, picks up the ball and tosses it back. Then changes direction to retrieve a ball rolled to the opposite side and does the same.

Player must stay in a good down position with the back straight and knees bent.

Go back and forth for 1 minute. Minimum three rounds. Maximum 7 rounds.

The Drill:
Forehand High/Low

comment:

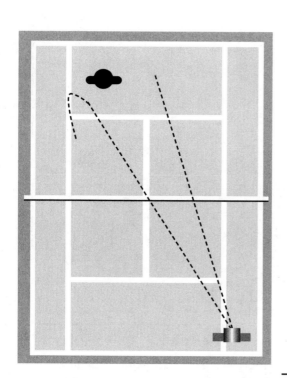

The Purpose:
Improves a player's offense ability to handle balls on the rise or on the drop. Each type of ball presents a different type of opportunity as well as a different type of risk. Improves consistency.

The Practice
Player rallys with coach or practice partner hitting the opposite shot that comes at them.

If it's high then the player drives the ball low over the net.

If it's low then the player hits a higher heavier ball over the net.

The Drill:

Hit Big or Go Home

comment:

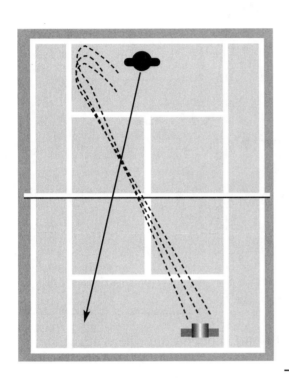

The Purpose:

Improves the ability of a player to end points by taking forehands from the middle of the court on the rise.

The Practice:

Player stands inside the baseline.

Coach feeds topspin style shots that bounce low to medium height around the middle of the court.

Player practices taking everything as a forehand and on the rise and hitting it into the open court.

Coach changes court positions every twenty balls or so.

The Drill:

Everything Inside-Out

comment:

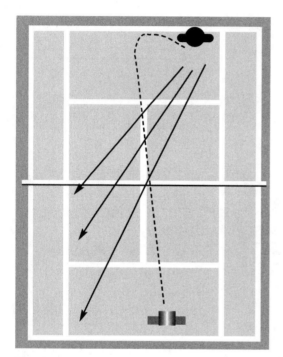

The Purpose:

Improves movement around softly hit shots hit anywhere near the back-hand side.

The Situation:

Your opponent has floated or hit medium speed topspin to your backhand. The slower shot gives you time to move around it and hit your forehand inside out to the opposite sideline either for a winner or as a setup. Use different wrist snaps according to the ball height.

The Practice:

Coach feeds an arching ball towards the backhand

Player moves around the ball to get into position for an inside-out shot

Player hits 10 balls to deepest cone target then 10 balls to the next target and so on until all four targeted areas have been hit.

Coach feeds to a new backhand area making the player move more

Repeat 15-20 minutes hitting to different sideline areas

The Drill:
Inside-Out—-Not!

comment:

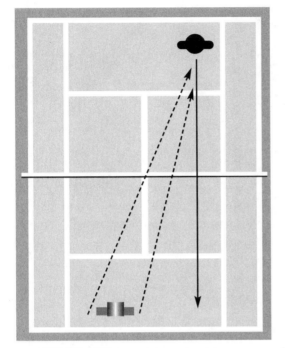

The Purpose:
Improves the ability of a player to move the ball from corner to corner and catch opponents cheating one way. Helps improve footwork and ball striking while on the move.

The Situation:
You've just it two or three inside out forehands for winners and your opponent has hit a floater once again to your backhand side. This time as you move around the backhand as your opponent takes a cheater step towards the inside out angle that you've been hitting. So this time you open up your stance early and pull the ball down the sideline either flat or with excessive topspin.

The Practice:
Coach feeds balls to backhand side of player
Player moves around the ball with the same set up as the inside out forehand
Player steps into an open stance at the last second and hits the ball down the sideline
Player hits 10 shots from various feeds to two different depths, service line and baseline
Repeat 15-20 minutes

The Drill:
The Corner Slap

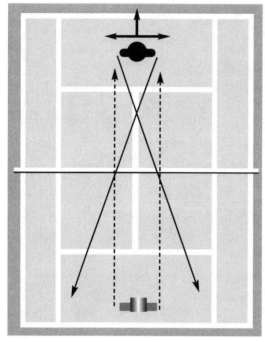

comment:

The Purpose:
Improves a player's ability to end points on high balls hit inside the base-line. This shot emphasizes the windshield wiper wrist snap.

The Situation:
Your opponent has hit a high bouncing topspin shot to the middle of the court. You move up but don't have time to catch it on the rise so you let the ball rise above your shoulders so you can hit a flat slap shot forehand into the corner with a little inside out spin that you put on the high ball by pronating your wrist through the ball. This is also known as the windshield wiper shot because of how your racquet moves across the back of the ball and the front of your body.

The Practice:
Coach stands middle baseline and feeds heavy topspin to the middle service line area
Player moves in to take ball as a high forehand
Player hits 10 shots to right side corner
Player hits 10 shots to left side corner
Repeat 15-20 minutes

The Drill:
Backhand—One-Sided Wonder

comment:

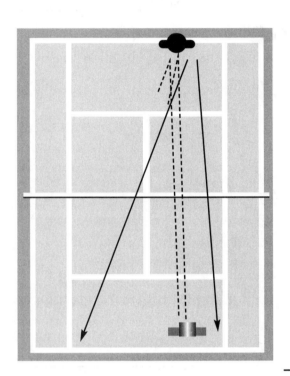

The Purpose:
Improves the ability of a player to alternate their shots to keep a player on the hook once an advantage has been gained.

The Situation:
You've hit an aggressive shot that has the opponent on the hook. With each shot that comes back to you've gained a little advantage and your opponent is scrambling in recovery. If you continue to change the direction of the ball you will soon have your opponent worked off the court for good.

The Practice:
Player stands in the backhand corner.

Coach feeds or hits different style shots with a variety of speeds and spins into the player's backhand corner.

Player practices alternating shots from side to side hitting the right shot according to the shot type.

The Drill:
Backhand Open Stance Angles

comment:

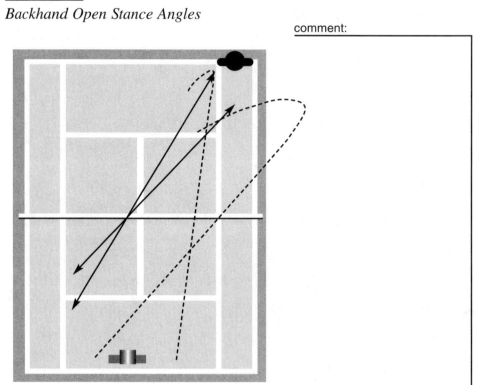

The Purpose:
Improves the ability of a player to alternate their shots to keep a player on the hook once an advantage has been gained.

The Situation:
You've hit an aggressive shot that has the opponent on the hook. With each shot that comes back to you've gained a little advantage and your opponent is scrambling in recovery. If you continue to change the direction of the ball you will soon have your opponent worked off the court for good.

The Practice:
Player stands in the backhand corner.

Coach feeds or hits different style shots with a variety of speeds and spins into the player's backhand corner.

Player practices alternating shots from side to side hitting the right shot according to the shot type.

The Drill:

Returns—Serves from the service line

comment:

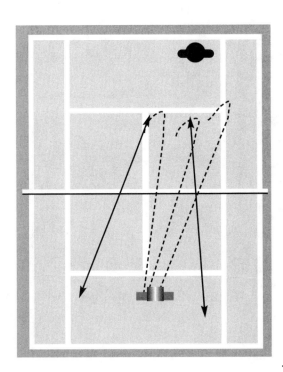

The Purpose:
Improves hand eye coordination and racquet speed wrist snap.

The Situation:
Returning fast well placed serves more consistently.

The Practice:
Coach serves from service line.
Player takes normal return position at the baseline.
Player practices taking returns on the rise.

The Drill:
The 7 volley zones

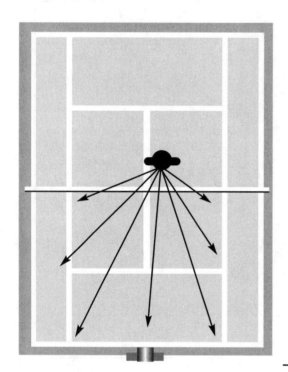

comment:

The Purpose:
Improves the ability of a player to place his or her volleys using both feel and power.

The Situation:
You've hit an aggressive approach shot and come to the net but your opponent has hit a neutralizing shot in response so that you can't power the ball away for a winner. You instead must be able to place your volley away from your opponent and try and set yourself up.

The Practice:
Player stands in midcourt and hits an approach shot down the line.
Coach feeds or hits a variety of shots so that the player can execute volleys to all seven zones.
Player stays at the net until all 7 zones have been hit and then returns to midcourt.

The Drill:

Serves—The 8 cones

comment:

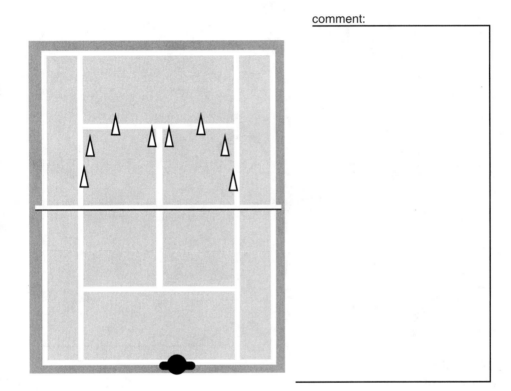

The Purpose:

Improves the ability of a player to place all three types of serves into the different zones of the service boxes.

The Practice:

Player takes normal serving position.

Starting with the flat serve the player hits 5 balls at each cone then switches to a slice serve and then to a kick serve.

The Drill:
Futuremetrics—Power and Agility Course

comment:

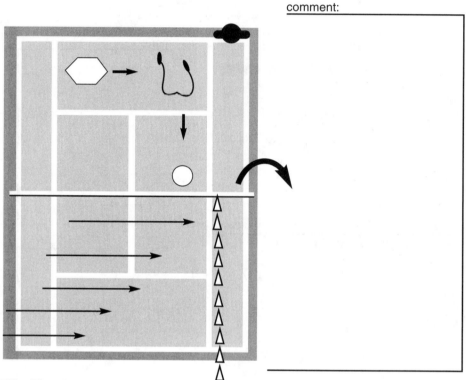

The Purpose:
Improves the power and agility of a player when performed in a Futuremetrics style training program.

The Practice:
Player starts at the hexagon station.

Hexagon jumps-jump in and out of hexagon going across each side. (3 times around)

Jump rope station—15 one leg jumps each leg.

10-10lbs. Medicine ball overhead throws. —Using a wall or pole have player touch the back of their neck and then throw as high as they can on the wall.

10 cones 2-step with shuffle return—3 times through—set up 10 cones 3 heels to toe steps apart. Player hops through putting down two steps between each cone and then side shuffling back to start.

35 feet 5-line suicide sprint. (Each line 7ft apart)

The Drill:

The Wheel Run

comment:

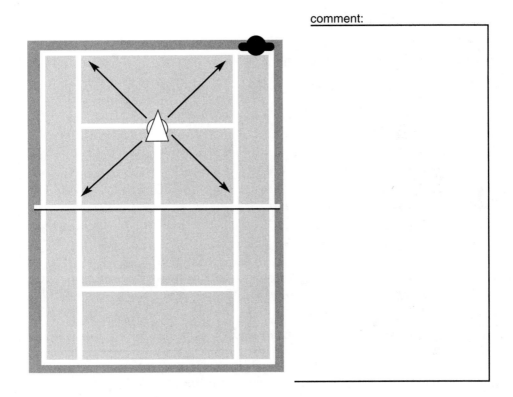

The Purpose:
Improves a player's quickness and overall mobility around the court.

The Practice:
Player sprints to a cone placed at the service line T, touches it and then proceeds to the next corner of the court, touches there and then proceeds back to the cone again.

Player follows this pattern until he or she reaches the corner of the court where they started.

Timed less than 16 seconds.

The DRILL

Crosscourt based game—Cross/Down the line

comment:

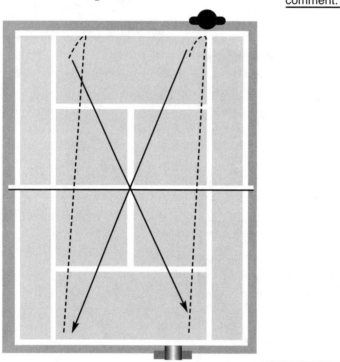

The Purpose:
Improves the ability of a player to change the direction of a ball while on the move.

The Situation:
Your opponent has hit a crosscourt shot but it isn't deep enough or lacks penetrating speed so you take the ball as early as you can and drive it down the line. Your opponent then retrieves your shot and hits another crosscourt.

The Practice:
Player stands in the backhand corner.

Coach or practice partner hits a crosscourt shot to the forehand side to start the drill pattern.

Player practices hitting all crosscourt shots with topspin for control and practices hitting all down the line shots flat for winners.

Switch from hitting crosscourt to down the line every 5 balls.

The Drill:

Hit everything crosscourt

comment:

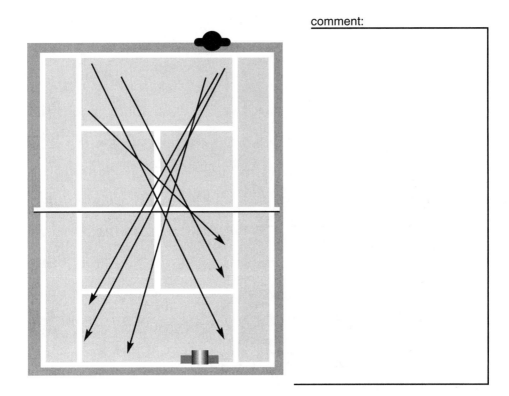

The Purpose:

Improves the ability of a player to hit to certain areas of the court on any type of ball. Improves focus and patients. Helps develop mental game skills.

The Practice:

Coach feeds or hits different style shots with a variety of speeds and spins all around the court.

Player focuses on one game plan, to hit every shot crosscourt no matter where it is on the court and no matter where the opponent is standing.

The Drill:
3 Cone Sprint and Shuffle

comment:

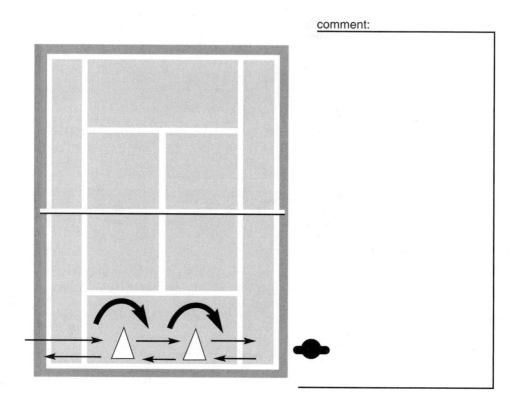

The Purpose:
Improves a player's footwork and leg strength.

The Practice

Put 2 cones in a row on the middle of the baseline 3 yards apart.
Player starts at the right doubles sideline and sprints to the first cone, then does a crossover step over the cone and shuffles to the next cone and does another crossover step and then sprints to the other sideline and then comes back through the course.

MORE DRILLS:

The Drill:

The Purpose:

The Practice:

NOTES:

MORE DRILLS:

The Drill:

The Purpose:

The Practice:

NOTES:

MORE DRILLS:

The Drill:

The Purpose:

The Practice:

NOTES: